Air Fryer Cookbook for Beginners UK 2021

The Ultimate Air Fryer Guide with 100+ Simple and Delicious Recipes for Better Health and Making Great Meals.

Author: Michael Williams

Legal Notice:

Copyright 2021 by Michael Williams - All rights reserved.

This document is geared towards providing exact and reliable information regarding the topic and issue covered. The publication is sold on the idea that the publisher is not required to render an accounting, officially permitted, or otherwise, qualified services. If advice is necessary, legal or professional, a practiced individual in the profession should be ordered.

From a Declaration of Principles which was accepted and approved equally by a Committee of the American Bar Association and a Committee of Publishers and Associations.

Legal Notes:

In no way is it legal to reproduce, duplicate, or transmit any part of this document by either electronic means or in printed format. Recording of this publication is strictly prohibited and any storage of this document is not allowed unless with written permission from the publisher. All rights reserved.

The information provided herein is stated to be truthful and consistent, in that any liability, in terms of inattention or otherwise, by any usage or abuse of any policies, processes, or directions contained within is the solitary and utter responsibility of the recipient reader. Under no circumstances will any legal responsibility or blame be held against the publisher for any reparation, damages, or monetary loss due to the information herein, either directly or indirectly. Respective authors own all copyrights not held by the publisher.

Disclaimer Notice:

The information herein is offered for informational purposes solely and is universal as so. The presentation of the information is without a contract or any type of guarantee assurance. Readers acknowledge that the author is not engaging in the rendering of legal, financial, medical or professional advice. Please consult a licensed professional before attempting any techniques outlined in this book.

The trademarks that are used are without any consent, and the publication of the trademark is without permission or backing by the trademark owner. All trademarks and brands within this book are for clarifying purposes only and are the owned by the owners themselves, not affiliated with this document.

Fundamentals of Air Fryer Cooking 7

Different Types of Air Fryers 8

Health Benefits of Air Frying 9

Is it healthier to cook in an Air Fryer or a Conventional Oven? ...... **Error! Bookmark not defined.**

Top 8 Tips to Use Your Air Fryer Like A Pro 12

    French Toast 14

    Cheesy Toasts with Egg & Bacon 15

    Bacon & Egg Cups 16

    Spinach & Mozzarella Cups 17

    Chicken Omelet 18

    Tofu & Mushroom Omelet 19

    Chicken & Broccoli Quiche 20

    Trout Frittata 21

    Sausage & Capsicum Casserole 22

    Potato Rosti 23

    Pumpkin Pancakes 24

    Banana Bread 25

    Date Bread 26

    Oat & Raisin Muffins 27

    Savory Carrot Muffins 28

Poultry Recipes 29

    Roasted Chicken 29

    Spicy Chicken Legs 30

    Glazed Chicken Drumsticks 31

    Crispy Chicken Thighs 32

    Oat Crusted Chicken Breasts 33

    Bacon-Wrapped Chicken Breast 34

    Breaded Chicken Cutlets 35

    Simple Turkey Breast 36

- Glazed Turkey Breast ... 37
- Zesty Turkey Legs ... 38
- Turkey Rolls ... 39
- Turkey Meatloaf ... 40
- Turkey Stuffed Capsicums ... 41
- Herbed Duck Legs ... 42
- Buttered Duck Breasts ... 43

Red Meat Recipes ... 44
- Buttered Rib-Eye Steak ... 44
- Bacon-Wrapped Filet Mignon ... 45
- Sweet & Sour Short Ribs ... 46
- Parmesan Meatballs ... 47
- Beef Taco Wraps ... 48
- Glazed Pork Shoulder ... 49
- BBQ Pork Ribs ... 50
- Breaded Pork Chops ... 51
- Pork Rolls ... 52
- Glazed Ham ... 53
- Herbed Leg of Lamb ... 54
- Spiced Lamb Steaks ... 55
- Pesto Rack of Lamb ... 56
- Simple Lamb Chops ... 57
- Mustard Lamb Chops ... 58

Fish & Seafood Recipes ... 59
- Spicy Salmon ... 59
- Maple Salmon ... 60
- Cod Parcel ... 61
- Ranch Tilapia ... 62
- Glazed Halibut ... 63
- Sesame Seed Tuna ... 64
- Shrimp Scampi ... 65

    Shrimp Kabobs 66
    Prawn Burgers 67
    Scallops with Spinach 68
Vegetarian Recipes 69
    Hasselback Potatoes 69
    Parmesan Brussels Sprout 70
    Feta Spinach 71
    Mushroom with Peas 72
    Broccoli with Cauliflower 73
    Stuffed Tomatoes 74
    Oats & Beans Stuffed Capsicums 75
    Tofu with Cauliflower 76
    Beans & Veggie Burgers 77
    Veggie Rice 78
Snacks Recipes 79
    Roasted Cashews 79
    Apple Chips 80
    French Fries 81
    Onion Rings 82
    Mozzarella Sticks 83
    Broccoli Poppers 84
    Chicken Nuggets 85
    Buffalo Chicken Wings 86
    Bacon-Wrapped Shrimp 87
    Crispy Prawns 88
Dessert Recipes 89
    Stuffed Apples 89
    Brownie Muffins 90
    Shortbread Fingers 91
    Lava Cake 92
    Butter Cake 93

- Simple Cheesecake 94
- Cherry Clafoutis 95
- Apple Crumble 96
- Fudge Brownies 97
- Raisin Bread Pudding 98

Keto Air Fryer Recipes 99
- Parsley Soufflé 99
- Ham Casserole 100
- Pumpkin Bread 101
- 2-Ingredients Chicken Breasts 102
- Parmesan Chicken Thighs 103
- Stuffed Chicken Breasts 104
- Turkey Feta Burgers 105
- Buttered Fillet Mignon 106
- Herbed Beef Roast 107
- Parmesan Pork Chops 108
- Pork Taco Casserole 109
- Almond Coated Rack of Lamb 110
- Buttered Trout 111
- Haddock with Pesto 112
- Cheesy Shrimp 113
- Scallops with Capers Sauce 114
- Jalapeño Poppers 115
- Cranberry Muffins 116
- Brownie Cake 117
- Cheesecake Bites 118

Fundamentals of Air Fryer Cooking

Congrats on deciding to embark on an Air Fryer exploration journey! The air fryer is among the world's newest ground-breaking kitchen appliances that, dare I say it, will change your cooking experiences forever. Gone are the days of slaving over a fryer, now you can enjoy food that's crispy on the outside and juicy on the inside using one extraordinary appliance. This air fryer is a more sophisticated and developed version than the previous air fryer ovens of past years.

Since its introduction, the air fryer has garnered a huge reputation for producing delicious meals using hot air circulation technology that distributes scorching hot air inside your air fryer oven with the help of convection fans. As you can imagine, this aids in making the cooking process faster and helps to ensure that you can produce delicious dishes such as crispy fried fries with very little oil.

What's even better is that most air fryers are multi-cooker kitchen appliances. Many of which features 6 to 7 different cooking modes. A typical Air Fryer will be able to carry just about dry cooking method you can think of, including, but limited to, dehydrating, baking, roasting, frying, and grilling. On top of this, it also saves a ton of space on your kitchen countertop.

The largest advantage, however, is that it comes with an expanded capacity which means you will be able to air fry larger quantities of food at once.

Different Types of Air Fryers

There are various kinds of air fryers, every single diverse brand, and with various top picks.
- Size matters, particularly if you're expecting to sustain a group of four to six hungry individuals.
- If you're thinking about what size of air fryer to get my advice is the 3-4 qt sizes for 2-3 individuals (or if it's all the same to you cooking numerous bunches) and the 5-6 qt for groups of 4-6 (you'll despite everything cook somethings in clumps, yet not as much as the smaller air fryers).
- We're for the most part cooking for two during the bustling weeknights, and the 3 qt size fryers are extraordinary for us.

Here are a few of the top models that have dominated over the past few years:
1. Krups Easy Fry Deluxe Digital Air Fryer 4.2 L
2. NuWave Bravo XL Smart Oven
3. Instant Vortex Plus Air Fryer Oven
4. NuWave Brio Digital Air Fryer 6 Quart
5. Dash Compact Air Fryer
6. Farberware 3.2-Quart Digital Oil-Less Fryer
7. Black and Decker 2L Purifry Air Fryer
8. Philips Air fryer XXL
9. GoWise 8-in-1 Air Fryer XL 5.9 Qt.
10. Ninja Air Fryer
11. Breville Smart Oven Air
12. Krups Fry Delight
13. Cuisinart Air fryer Toaster Oven
14. Power Air Fryer XL
15. Black and Decker Crisp 'N Bake Air Fry Toaster Oven
16. Cuisinart Compact Air Fryer
17. Oster DuraCeramic Air Fryer

No matter what type of Air Fryer you opt to utilize, it will offer you a myriad of benefits. We'll take a look at a few of these benefits in the next section.

Health Benefits of Air Frying

Believe it or not, air fried foods require little to no oil at all. Ingredients are cooked with the aid of hot air, tasting as amazing as if oil was used. You no longer have to worry about greasy dish stains or fingers, as oil is not necessary to get the job done. Although oil can be used in the air fryer for frying, it is not a common occurrence for it to be used.
When oil is used, direct application to foods is best, as opposed to pouring lots of oil, risking damage to the appliance. The concept of common foods being made healthier without oil is appealing to those on fat-blasting diets. Eliminating oil also means that your cleaning job is easier. If using oil to prepare a meal, use with homemade foods (as opposed to pre-heated foods). The manual in the Air Fryer informs you of the oils that you can use. As you can imagine, this in turn leads to a myriad of benefits, both concerning your health and lifestyle as a whole. These include, but are certainly not limited to:

- **Healthier Foods**

Nothing beats the healthy results of cooking with the Air Fryer appliance. It is uniquely designed to operate without oil, reducing fats in foods by up to eighty percent. Losing weight has never been so easy, as the Air Fryer couples your need for indulgence with healthier alternatives. Apart from offering you foods lower in saturated fats and calories, the Air Fryer is multi-functional in baking, roasting and grilling. No doubt, the Air Fryer is the best tool for a changed lifestyle, as it is an appliance that makes healthy living much simpler.

- **Aiding in Weight Loss**

Obesity has been tied to many chronic illnesses, including hypertension, and though using an air fryer was not initially intended to be used for weight loss, it has also been proven to help promote weight control due to limited use of oil during cooking and allowing you to avoid deep frying.

- **Avoiding Heart Disease & High Cholesterol**

Using an air fryer restricts the need to deep fry in tons of unhealthy oils and other saturated fats that are largely associated with cardiovascular problems and high cholesterol. It also encourages you to eat more fibrous foods that can stand up to dehydration, frying and/or roasting that promote the reduction of plaque in, and around your arteries.

- **Maintains Nutritional Values from The Food That's Fried**

When you use a traditional deep fryer, food is often fried in large amounts of bad fat that soaks into your food and the beneficial nutrients and vitamins are destroyed. The Air Fryer removes the large amount of oil from the equation by circulating the hot air into the cooking chamber. Due to this it protects the essential vitamins and nutrients in your food and never adds bad fats in it.

Along with these, air frying also carries additional benefits such as:

- **Easy to clean up**

We all know that frying can attract a hefty mess, whether you use a pan or deep fryer. The remnants of oil are hard to discard, and still, it is difficult to clean up such a slippery mess.

- **Great for Baking**

You might ask why one with a fully decked kitchen would need an air-fryer with additional functions. Well, air fryers use convectional heating, whereas many household ovens use conventional heating. Convectional heating, which is the better alternative, is good for dishes such as roasted chicken and baked goods.

- **Quick Meals**

If you're always on the go, the Air Fryer is perfect for you. Within minutes, it prepares crispy fries or chicken tenders. With french fries taking an average of 12 minutes to prepare, you don't have to worry about long waits or the frustration they bring.

- **Multi-Purpose Cooking Appliance**

Most air fryers offer a 7 in 1 cooking appliance. Air fryer performs operations of 7 different cooking appliances allowing you to fry, bake, roast, dehydrate and more.

Top 5 Tips to Use Your Air Fryer Like A Pro

Now that you know a bit more about using the Air Fryer, let's explore a few tips, and tricks that will make your Air Fryer journey a bit easier.

1. **Leave enough space in your basket to shake or flip**

As with a traditional deep fryer, your food will need space to be fully surrounded by the cooking source. A normal deep fryer cooks by having hot oil penetrate each particle of food. The same principle applies to the Air Fryer. In order to perfectly cook your food items, air has to fully surround each particle. To support this concept, it is recommended that you periodically shake the Air Fryer basket to avoid compression or getting the food stuck together.

2. **Avoid overcrowding your Air Fryer basket**

Overloading your fryer can hinder the cooking process. So, instead of packing it all in at once and winding up with underdone food, consider cooking in batches.

3. **Consider spraying your food with oil prior to cooking**

Though not a requirement in all cases, a splash of oil can in fact go a long way on the road to crispy and delicious meal. An easy way to do this is to invest in an oil spritzer that will allow you to simply spray the food you are about to cook.

4. **Take the steps required to keep your fryer clean and dry**

This comes into play from the moment you remove your new appliance from the box all the way through the cooking process. As such, if you find that the food you are preparing requires you to coat or bread the item prior to frying, be sure to shake off any excess breading or liquid before adding it to your air fryer basket. This excess coating material can drip or fall onto the bottom of your appliance and burn making it harder to clean.

The same can be said about high fat foods that may melt onto the bottom of your fryer and create a smoky mess the next time it is used. To avoid this, consider cleaning your fryer as soon as it is cool enough to touch after each use. Alternately, you can opt to line the bottom of your air fryer basket with high heat parchment paper or foil before cooking. Doing this will aid in making your air fryer life significantly easier when it's time to clean. Alternately you can opt to use parchment paper. Be sure to top your paper with the mesh basket as the air will blow it out of place, and the high circulating temperatures can cause it to become inflamed.

5. Utilize all your fryer's functions to get the most from the appliance

Your air fryer can be used for so much more than just frying. In fact, a typical air fryer will be able to carry just about dry cooking method you can think of; dehydrating, baking, roasting, frying, and grilling. Most models even allow you to cook without using the fryer basket. This allows you to take full advantage of the space available in air fryer or even to use it as a mini fryer. Be sure to consult your manual to be sure your models allow you to cook without the basket before doing so.

BREAKFAST RECIPES

French Toast

Serves: 2
Prep Time: 10 mins.
Cooking Time: 3 mins.

Ingredients:

- 2 eggs
- 3 tablespoons sugar
- 1/8 teaspoon vanilla extract
- 60 ml evaporated milk
- 2 teaspoons olive oil
- 4 bread slices

Directions:
Set the temperature of Air Fryer to 160 degrees C and preheat for 5 minutes. Grease an air fryer pan and insert in the Air Fryer while heating. In a large bowl, mix together all ingredients except for bread slices. Coat the bread slices with egg mixture evenly. After preheating, arrange the bread slices into the prepared pan. Slide the pan in Air Fryer and set the time for 6 minutes. Flip the slices once after 3 minutes. Serve warm.

Calories: 262   **Protein: 9.1g**   **Carbs: 30.7g**   **Fat: 12.1g**

Cheesy Toasts with Egg & Bacon

Serves: 4

Prep Time: 15 mins.

Cooking Time: 4 mins.

Ingredients:

- 4 bread slices
- 113 grams ricotta cheese, crumbled
- Ground black pepper, as required
- 4 cooked bacon slices, crumbled
- 1 garlic clove, minced
- ¼ teaspoon lemon zest
- 2 hard-boiled eggs, peeled and chopped

Directions:

In a food processor, add the garlic, ricotta, lemon zest and black pepper and pulse until smooth. Spread ricotta mixture over each bread slices evenly. Set the temperature of Air Fryer to 180 degrees C and preheat for 5 minutes. Arrange the bread slices into the greased air fryer basket. Slide the basket in Air Fryer and set the time for 4 minutes. Remove from Air Fryer and transfer the bread slices onto serving plates. Top with egg and bacon pieces and serve.

Calories: 416 **Protein:** 27.2g **Carbs:** 11.2g **Fat:** 29.3g

Bacon & Egg Cups

Serves: 2

Prep Time: 10 mins.

Cooking Time: 8 mins.

Ingredients:

- 1 cooked bacon slice, chopped
- 2 tablespoons milk
- 1 teaspoon marinara sauce
- 1 tablespoon fresh parsley, chopped
- 2 eggs
- Ground black pepper, as required
- 1 tablespoon Parmesan cheese, grated
- 2 bread slices, toasted and buttered

Directions:

Set the temperature of Air Fryer to 180 degrees C and preheat for 5 minutes. Divide the bacon into 2 ramekins. Crack 1 egg in each ramekin over the bacon. Pour the milk over eggs and sprinkle with black pepper. Top with marinara sauce, followed by the Parmesan cheese. Arrange the ramekins into the air fryer basket. Slide the basket in Air Fryer and set the time for 8 minutes. Remove from Air Fryer and sprinkle with parsley. Serve hot alongside the bread slices.

Calories: 215   **Protein: 14.9g**   **Carbs: 13.1g**   **Fat: 11.4g**

Spinach & Mozzarella Cups

Serves: 2

Prep Time: 10 mins.

Cooking Time: 10 mins.

Ingredients:

- 2 large eggs
- 3 tablespoons frozen spinach, thawed
- Salt and ground black pepper, as required
- 2 tablespoons half-and-half
- 4 teaspoons mozzarella cheese, grated

Directions:
Grease 2 ramekins. In each prepared ramekin, crack 1 egg. Divide the half-and-half, spinach, cheese, salt and black pepper and each ramekin and gently stir to combine, without breaking the yolks. Set the temperature of Air Fryer to 165 degrees C and preheat for 5 minutes. Arrange the ramekins into the air fryer basket. Slide the basket in Air Fryer and set the time for 10 minutes. Serve warm.

Calories: 251　　**Protein:** 22.8g　　**Carbs:** 3.1g　　**Fat:** 16.7g

Chicken Omelet

Serves: 2

Prep Time: 10 mins.

Cooking Time: 17 mins.

Ingredients:

- 1 teaspoon butter
- ½ jalapeño pepper, seeded and chopped
- Salt and ground black pepper, as required
- 1 onion, chopped
- 3 eggs
- 35 grams cooked chicken, shredded

Directions:
In a frying pan, melt the butter over medium heat and sauté the onion for about 4-5 minutes. Add in the jalapeño pepper and sauté for about 1 minute. Add the chicken and stir to combine. Remove from the heat and set aside. In a bowl, mix together the eggs, salt, and black pepper. Place the chicken mixture into a greased baking pan. Pour the egg mixture over chicken mixture. Set the temperature of Air Fryer to 180 degrees C and preheat for 5 minutes. Arrange the baking pan into the air fryer basket. Slide the basket in Air Fryer and set the time for 10 minutes. Serve hot.

Calories: 161   **Protein: 14.1g**   **Carbs: 5.9g**   **Fat: 9.1g**

Tofu & Mushroom Omelet

Serves: 2

Prep Time: 15 mins.

Cooking Time: 29 mins.

Ingredients:
- 2 teaspoons canola oil
- 1 garlic clove, minced
- 99 grams fresh mushrooms, sliced
- 3 eggs, beaten
- ¼ of onion, chopped
- 226 grams silken tofu, pressed and sliced
- Salt and ground black pepper, as required

Directions:
Set the temperature of Air Fryer to 180 degrees C and preheat for 5 minutes. In an air fryer pan, add the oil, onion, and garlic. Slide the pan in Air Fryer and set the time for 29 minutes. After 4 minutes of cooking and remove the pan from Air Fryer. In the pan, add the tofu, mushrooms, red pepper flakes, salt and black pepper. Top with the beaten eggs evenly. While cooking, poke the eggs after every 8 minutes. Remove the pan from Air Fryer and serve hot.

Calories: 224   **Protein: 17.9g**   **Carbs: 6.6g**   **Fat: 14.4g**

Chicken & Broccoli Quiche

Serves: 8

Prep Time: 15 mins.

Cooking Time: 12 mins.

Ingredients:

- 1 frozen ready-made pie crust
- 1 egg
- 3 tablespoons whipping cream
- 18 grams boiled broccoli, chopped
- ½ tablespoon olive oil
- 43 grams cheddar cheese, grated
- Salt and ground black pepper, as required
- 35 grams cooked chicken, chopped

Directions:
Lightly grease 2 small pie pans with olive oil. Cut 2 (12-centimeters) rounds from the pie crust. Arrange 1 pie crust round in each pie pan and gently press in the bottom and sides. In a bowl, mix together the egg, cheese, cream, salt, and black pepper. Pour the egg mixture over dough base and top with the broccoli and chicken. Set the temperature of Air Fryer to 200 degrees C and preheat for 5 minutes. Arrange the pie pans into the air fryer basket. Slide the basket in Air Fryer and set the time for 12 minutes. Remove the pie pans from Air Fryer and place onto a wire rack to cool for about 5 minutes before serving.

Calories: 166 **Protein:** 4.2g **Carbs:** 14.6g **Fat:** 10.4g

Trout Frittata

Serves: 4

Prep Time: 15 mins.

Cooking Time: 25 mins.

Ingredients:

- 2 tablespoons olive oil
- 6 eggs
- 2 tablespoons crème fraiche
- 3-4 tablespoons fresh dill, chopped
- 1 onion, sliced
- ½ tablespoon horseradish sauce
- 2 hot-smoked trout fillets, chopped

Directions:
In a frying pan, heat the oil over medium heat and sauté the onion for about 4-5 minutes. Remove from the heat and transfer the onion mixture into a baking dish. Set aside to cool slightly. Meanwhile, in a bowl, mix together the eggs, horseradish sauce, and crème fraiche. Place the egg mixture over the onion mixture, followed by trout. Set the temperature of Air Fryer to 160 degrees C and preheat for 5 minutes. Arrange the baking dish into the air fryer basket. Slide the basket in Air Fryer and set the time for 20 minutes. Serve hot.

Calories: 342 **Protein: 31.9g** **Carbs: 21.5g** **Fat: 21.6g**

Sausage & Capsicum Casserole

Serves: 6

Prep Time: 15 mins.

Cooking Time: 25 mins.

Ingredients:

- 1 teaspoon olive oil
- 455 grams ground sausage
- 30 grams onion, chopped
- 55 grams Colby Jack cheese, shredded
- ½ teaspoon garlic salt
- 1 capsicum, seeded and chopped
- 8 eggs, beaten
- 1 teaspoon fennel seed

Directions:
In a skillet, heat the oil over medium heat and cook the sausage for about 4-5 minutes. Add the capsicum and onion and cook for about 4-5 minutes. Remove from the heat and transfer the sausage mixture into a bowl to cool slightly. In a baking pan, place the sausage mixture and top with the cheese, followed by the beaten eggs, fennel seed and garlic salt. Set the temperature of Air Fryer to 200 degrees C and preheat for 5 minutes. Arrange the baking pan into the air fryer basket. Slide the basket in Air Fryer and set the time for 15 minutes. Cut into equal-sized wedges and serve hot.

Calories: 391 **Protein:** 24.4g **Carbs:** 2.5g **Fat:** 31.1g

Potato Rosti

Serves: 2

Prep Time: 15 mins.

Cooking Time: 15 mins.

Ingredients:

- 1 teaspoon olive oil
- 1 tablespoon fresh chives, chopped
- Salt and ground black pepper, as required
- 99 grams smoked salmon, cut into slices
- 226 grams russet potatoes, peeled and roughly grated
- 2 tablespoons sour cream

Directions:
In a bowl, mix together the potato, herbs, red pepper flakes, salt and black pepper. Arrange the potato mixture into the baking pan and shape it into an even circle. Set the temperature of Air Fryer to 180 degrees C and preheat for 5 minutes. Arrange the baking pan into the air fryer basket. Slide the basket in Air Fryer and set the time for 15 minutes. Remove from Air Fryer and cut the potato rosti into wedges. Top with the sour cream and smoked salmon slices and serve immediately.

Calories: 182 **Protein:** 11.4g **Carbs:** 18.3g **Fat:** 7.1g

Pumpkin Pancakes

Serves: 4

Prep Time: 10 mins.

Cooking Time: 122 mins.

Ingredients:

- 1 square puff pastry
- 1 small egg, beaten
- 3 tablespoons pumpkin filling

Directions:
Roll out a puff pastry square and layer it with pumpkin pie filling, leaving about 0.62-centimeters space around the edges. Cut it into 8 equal-sized square pieces and coat the edges with beaten egg. Arrange the squares into a greased baking pan. Set the temperature of Air Fryer to 180degrees C and preheat for 5 minutes. Arrange the baking pan into the air fryer basket. Slide the basket in Air Fryer and set the time for 12 minutes. Serve warm.

Calories: 109 **Protein:** 2.4g **Carbs:** 9.8g **Fat:** 6.7g

Banana Bread

Serves: 8

Prep Time: 10 mins.

Cooking Time: 20 mins.

Ingredients:

- 200 grams flour
- 1 teaspoon baking soda
- 1 teaspoon ground cinnamon
- 120 milliliters milk
- 3 bananas, peeled and sliced
- 85 grams sugar
- 1 teaspoon baking powder
- 1 teaspoon salt
- 120 milliliter olive oil

Directions:
In a bowl of a stand mixer, add all the ingredients and mix well. Place the mixture into a greased loaf pan. Set the temperature of air fryer to 165 degrees C and preheat for 5 minutes. Arrange the loaf pan into the air fryer basket. Slide the basket in Air Fryer and set the time for 20 minutes. Remove from air fryer and place the pan onto a wire rack for about 10-15 minutes. Carefully invert the bread onto a wire rack to cool completely before slicing. Cut the bread into desired sized slices and serve.

Calories: 301   **Protein:** 3.6g   **Carbs:** 41.1g   **Fat:** 14.9g

Date Bread

Serves: 10

Prep Time: 15 mins.

Cooking Time: 22 mins.

Ingredients:

- 370 grams dates, pitted and chopped
- 240milliliter hot water
- 85 grams brown sugar
- 1 teaspoon baking soda
- 1 egg
- 56½ grams butter
- 190 grams flour
- 1 teaspoon baking powder
- ½ teaspoon salt

Directions:
In a large bowl, add the dates, butter and top with the hot water. Set aside for about 5 minutes. In a separate bowl, mix together the flour, brown sugar, baking powder, baking soda, and salt. In the same bowl of dates, add the flour mixture and egg and mix well. Set the temperature of Air Fryer to 170 degrees C and preheat for 5 minutes. Place the mixture into a greased loaf pan. Arrange the pan into the air fryer basket. Slide the basket in Air Fryer and set the time for 22 minutes. Remove from Air Fryer and place the pan onto a wire rack for about 10-15 minutes. Carefully invert the bread onto the wire rack to cool completely cool before slicing. Cut the bread into desired sized slices and serve.

Calories: 253   **Protein: 3.5g**   **Carbs: 50.9g**   **Fat: 5.4g**

Oat & Raisin Muffins

Serves: 4

Prep Time: 10 mins.

Cooking Time: 10 mins.

Ingredients:

- 65 grams flour
- 1/8 teaspoon baking powder
- 113 grams butter, softened
- ¼ teaspoon vanilla extract
- 25 grams rolled oats
- 65 grams powdered sugar
- 2 eggs
- 37½ grams raisins

Directions:
In a bowl, mix together the flour, oats, and baking powder. In another bowl, add the sugar and butter. Beat until you get the creamy texture. Then, add in the egg and vanilla extract and beat until well combined. Add the egg mixture into oat mixture and mix until just combined. Fold in the raisins. Set the temperature of Air Fryer to 180 degrees C and preheat for 5 minutes. Place the mixture into 4 greased muffin molds evenly. Arrange the molds into the air fryer basket. Slide the basket in Air Fryer and set the time for 10 minutes. Remove the muffin molds from Air Fryer and place onto a wire rack to cool for about 10 minutes. Carefully invert the muffins onto the wire rack to completely cool before serving.

Calories: 409 **Protein: 5.8g** **Carbs: 40.6g** **Fat: 25.7g**

Savory Carrot Muffins

Serves: 4

Prep Time: 15 mins.

Cooking Time: 7 mins.

Ingredients:

- 32½ grams whole-wheat flour
- ½ teaspoon baking powder
- ½ teaspoon dried parsley, crushed
- 140 grams plain yogurt
- 1 tablespoon vegetable oil
- 1 carrot, peeled and grated
- 198 grams Parmesan cheese, grated

- 32½ grams all-purpose flour
- 1/8 teaspoon baking soda
- ½ teaspoon salt
- 1 teaspoon vinegar
- 3 tablespoons cottage cheese, grated
- 2-4 tablespoons water (if needed)
- 25 grams walnuts, chopped

Directions:
In a large bowl, mix together the flours, baking powder, baking soda, parsley, and salt. In another large bowl, add the yogurt and vinegar and mix well. Add the cottage cheese and carrot and mix well. (Add some water if needed). Make a well in the center of the yogurt mixture. Slowly add the flour mixture in the well and mix until well combined. Place the mixture into 6 greased muffin molds and top with the Parmesan cheese and walnuts. Set the temperature of Air Fryer to 180 degrees C and preheat for 5 minutes. Place the muffin molds into the air fryer basket. Slide the basket in Air Fryer and set the time for 7 minutes. Remove the muffin molds from Air Fryer and place onto a wire rack to cool for about 10 minutes. Carefully invert the muffins onto the wire rack to completely cool before serving.

Calories: 328　　　**Protein:** 22.2g　　　**Carbs:** 19.5g　　　**Fat:** 18.9g

Poultry Recipes

Roasted Chicken

Serves: 2

Prep Time: 10 mins.

Cooking Time: 40 mins.

Ingredients:
1 (680-grams) whole chicken
1 tablespoon olive oil

Salt and ground black pepper, as required

Directions:
Set the temperature of Air Fryer to 200 degrees C and preheat for 5 minutes. Grease the air fryer basket. Season the chicken with salt and black pepper. Place the chicken into the prepared air fryer basket. Slide the basket in Air Fryer and set the time for 35-40 minutes or until done completely. Remove from the Air Fryer and place the chicken onto a platter. With a sharp knife, cut the chicken into desired sized pieces and serve.

Calories: 698 **Protein:** 63.8g **Carbs:** 0g **Fat:** 49.6g

Spicy Chicken Legs

Serves: 4

Prep Time: 10 mins.

Cooking Time: 20 mins.

Ingredients:

- 4 chicken legs
- 1 teaspoon fresh ginger, minced
- Salt, as required
- 2 teaspoons red chili powder
- Ground black pepper, as required
- 3 tablespoons fresh lemon juice
- 1 teaspoon garlic, minced
- 4 tablespoons plain Greek yogurt
- 1 teaspoon ground cumin

Directions:

In a bowl, mix together the chicken legs, lemon juice, ginger, garlic and salt. Set aside for about 15 minutes. Meanwhile, in another bowl, mix together the yogurt and spices. Add the chicken legs and coat with the spice mixture generously. Cover the bowl and refrigerate for at least 10-12 hours. Set the temperature of Air Fryer to 230 degrees C and preheat for 5 minutes. Line the Air fryer basket with a piece of foil. Arrange chicken legs into the prepared air fryer basket. Slide the basket in Air Fryer and set the time for 18-20 minutes. Serve hot.

Calories: 507   **Protein: 75.1g**   **Carbs: 2.8g**   **Fat: 19.6g**

Glazed Chicken Drumsticks

Serves: 4

Prep Time: 15 mins.

Cooking Time: 22 mins.

Ingredients:

- 80 grams Dijon mustard
- 2 tablespoons olive oil
- 1 tablespoon fresh thyme, minced
- 4 (150-grams) boneless chicken drumsticks
- 1 tablespoon honey
- ½ tablespoon fresh rosemary, minced
- Salt and ground black pepper, as required

Directions:
In a bowl, add the mustard, honey, oil, herbs, salt, and black pepper and mix well. Add the drumsticks and coat with the mixture generously. Cover and refrigerate to marinate overnight. Set the temperature of Air Fryer to 160 degrees C and preheat for 5 minutes. Arrange the chicken drumsticks into the greased air fryer basket in a single layer. Slide the basket in Air Fryer and set the time for 12 minutes. After 12 minutes of cooking, set the temperature of Air Fryer to 180 degrees C for 5-10 more minutes. Serve hot.

Calories: 292 **Protein:** 25.1g **Carbs:** 5.8g **Fat:** 18.6g

Crispy Chicken Thighs

Serves: 4

Prep Time: 15 mins.

Cooking Time: 25 mins.

Ingredients:

- 65 grams all-purpose flour
- 1 teaspoon seasoning salt
- 4 (113-grams) skin-on chicken thighs
- 1½ tablespoons Cajun seasoning
- 1 egg

Directions:
In a shallow bowl, mix together the flour, Cajun seasoning, and salt. In another bowl, crack the egg and beat well. Coat each chicken thigh with the flour mixture, then dip into beaten egg and finally, coat with the flour mixture again. Shake off the excess flour thoroughly. Set the temperature of Air Fryer to 200 degrees C and preheat for 5 minutes. Arrange chicken thighs into the greased air fryer basket, skin side down. Slide the basket in Air Fryer and set the time for 25 minutes. Serve hot.

Calories: 290   **Protein: 35.8g**   **Carbs: 12.5g**   **Fat: 9.6g**

Oat Crusted Chicken Breasts

Serves: 2

Prep Time: 15 mins.

Cooking Time: 12 mins

Ingredients:

- 2 (150-grams) chicken breasts
- 75 grams oats
- 1 tablespoon fresh parsley
- Salt and ground black pepper, as required
- 2 tablespoons mustard powder
- 2 medium eggs

Directions:
Place the chicken breasts onto a cutting board and with a meat mallet, flatten each into an even thickness. Then, cut each breast in half. Sprinkle the chicken breasts with salt and black pepper and set aside. In a blender, add the oats, mustard powder, parsley, salt and black pepper and pulse until a coarse breadcrumb like mixture is formed. Transfer the oat mixture into a shallow bowl. In another bowl, crack the eggs and beat well. Coat the chicken breasts with oat mixture and then dip into beaten eggs and again coat with the oats mixture. Set the temperature of Air Fryer to 175 degrees C and preheat for 5 minutes. Grease a grill pan of Air Fryer. Arrange chicken breasts onto the prepared grill pan in a single layer. Slide the grill pan in Air Fryer and set the time for 12 minutes. Flip the chicken breasts once halfway through. Serve hot.

Calories: 429   **Protein: 45.1g**   **Carbs: 29.8g**   **Fat: 13.8g**

Bacon-Wrapped Chicken Breast

Serves: 4

Prep Time: 15 mins.

Cooking Time: 23 mins.

Ingredients:

- 1 tablespoon palm sugar
- 2 tablespoons fish sauce
- 2 (226-grams) chicken breasts, cut each breast in half horizontally
- 1½ teaspoon honey
- 6-7 Fresh basil leaves
- 2 tablespoons water
- Salt and ground black pepper, as required
- 12 bacon strips

Directions:

In a small heavy-bottomed pan, add palm sugar over medium-low heat and cook for about 2-3 minutes or until caramelized, stirring continuously. Add the basil, fish sauce and water and stir to combine. Remove from heat and transfer the sugar mixture into a large bowl. Sprinkle each chicken breast with salt and black pepper. Add the chicken pieces into the bowl of sugar mixture and coat generously. Refrigerate to marinate for about 4-6 hours. Wrap each chicken piece with 3 bacon strips. Coat each piece with honey slightly. Set the temperature of Air Fryer to 185 degrees C and preheat for 5 minutes. Arrange the chicken pieces into the air fryer basket. Slide the chicken pieces in Air Fryer and set the time for 20 minutes. Flip the chicken pieces once halfway through. Serve hot.

Calories: 365   **Protein: 30.2g**   **Carbs: 2.7g**   **Fat: 24.9g**

Breaded Chicken Cutlets

Serves: 4

Prep Time: 15 mins.

Cooking Time: 30 mins.

Ingredients:

- 97½ grams all-purpose flour
- 150 grams panko breadcrumbs
- 1 tablespoon mustard powder
- 4 (150-grams) skinless, boneless chicken cutlets
- 2 large eggs
- 27½ grams Parmesan cheese, grated
- Salt and ground black pepper, as required
- 1 lemon, cut into slices

Directions:

In a shallow bowl, place the flour. In a second bowl, crack the eggs and beat well. In a third bowl, mix together the breadcrumbs, cheese, mustard powder, salt, and black pepper. Season the chicken cutlets with salt and black pepper. Coat the chicken with flour, then dip into beaten eggs and finally coat with the breadcrumb mixture. Set the temperature of Air Fryer to 180 degrees C and preheat for 5 minutes. Arrange chicken cutlets into the greased air fryer basket in a single layer. Slide the basket in Air Fryer and set the time for 30 minutes. Remove from Air Fryer and transfer the chicken cutlets onto a serving platter. Serve hot with the topping of lemon slices.

Calories: 592 **Protein: 53.1g** **Carbs: 26.5g** **Fat: 19g**

Simple Turkey Breast

Serves: 10

Prep Time: 10 mins.

Cooking Time: 45 mins

Ingredients:

- 1 (3 kilograms 640 grams) bone-in turkey breast
- 2 tablespoons olive oil
- Salt and ground black pepper, as required

Directions:
Set the temperature of Air Fryer to 180 degrees C and preheat for 5 minutes. Sprinkle the turkey breast with salt and black pepper and drizzle with oil. Arrange turkey breast into the greased air fryer basket, skin side down. Slide the basket in Air Fryer and set the time for 45 minutes. After 20 minutes of cooking, flip the turkey breast. Remove from Air Fryer and place the turkey breast onto a cutting board for about 10 minutes before slicing. With a sharp knife, cut the turkey breast into desired sized slices and serve.

Calories: 720 **Protein:** 97.2g **Carbs:** 0g **Fat:** 9g

Glazed Turkey Breast

Serves: 8

Prep Time: 15 mins.

Cooking Time: 55 mins.

Ingredients:

- 1 teaspoon dried thyme, crushed
- ½ teaspoon smoked paprika
- Salt and ground black pepper, as required
- 2 teaspoons olive oil
- 2 tablespoons Dijon mustard
- ½ teaspoon dried sage, crushed
- ½ teaspoon smoked paprika
- 1 (2 kilograms 275 grams) boneless turkey breast
- 75 grams maple syrup
- 1 tablespoon butter, softened

Directions:

In a bowl, mix together the herbs, paprika, salt, and black pepper. Coat the turkey breast with oil. Now, coat the outer side of turkey breast with herb mixture. Set the temperature of Air Fryer to 175 degrees C and preheat for 5 minutes. Place turkey breast into the greased Air Fryer basket. Slide the basket in Air Fryer and set the time for 50 minutes. While cooking, flip the turkey breast once after 25 minutes and then after 12 minutes. Meanwhile, in a bowl, mix together the maple syrup, mustard, and butter. Remove the basket from Air Fryer and coat the turkey breast with glaze evenly. Slide the basket in Air Fryer and set the time for 5 minutes more. Remove from Air Fryer and place the turkey breast onto a cutting board for about 10 minutes before slicing. With a sharp knife, cut the turkey breast into desired sized slices and serve.

Calories: 328　　**Protein:** 70.5g　　**Carbs:** 7g　　**Fat:** 4.1g

Zesty Turkey Legs

Serves: 2

Prep Time: 15 mins.

Cooking Time: 30 mins.

Ingredients:

- 2 garlic cloves, minced
- 1 teaspoon fresh lime zest, finely grated
- 1 tablespoon fresh lime juice
- 2 turkey legs
- 1 tablespoon fresh rosemary, minced
- 2 tablespoons olive oil
- Salt and ground black pepper, as required

Directions:
In a large bowl, mix together the garlic, rosemary, lime zest, oil, lime juice, salt, and black pepper. Add the turkey legs and generously coat with marinade. Refrigerate to marinate for about 6-8 hours. Set the temperature of Air Fryer to 175 degrees C and preheat for 5 minutes. Arrange the turkey legs into the greased air fryer basket. Slide the basket in Air Fryer and set the time for 30 minutes. Flip the turkey legs once halfway through. Serve hot.

Calories: 458   **Protein: 44.6g**   **Carbs: 2.3g**   **Fat: 29.5g**

Turkey Rolls

Serves: 3

Prep Time: 20 mins.

Cooking Time: 40 mins.

Ingredients:

- 455 grams turkey breast fillet
- 1½ teaspoons ground cumin
- ½ teaspoon red chili powder
- 3 tablespoons fresh parsley, finely chopped
- 1 garlic clove, crushed
- 1 teaspoon ground cinnamon
- Salt, as required
- 2 tablespoons olive oil
- 1 small red onion, finely chopped

Directions:

Place the turkey fillet on a cutting board. Carefully cut horizontally along the length about 1/3 of the way from the top, stopping about 0.62-centimeters from the edge. Open this part to have a long piece of fillet. In a bowl, mix together the garlic, spices, and oil. In a small cup, reserve about 1 tablespoon of oil mixture. In the remaining oil mixture, add the parsley and onion and mix well. Coat the open side of fillet with onion mixture. Roll the fillet tightly from the short side. With a kitchen string, tie the roll at 3¾-centimeters intervals. Coat the outer side of roll with the reserved oil mixture. Set the temperature of Air Fryer to 180 degrees C and preheat for 5 minutes. Arrange the turkey roll into the air greased fryer basket. Slide the basket in Air Fryer and set the time for 40 minutes. Remove from Air Fryer and place the turkey roll onto a cutting board for about 5-10 minutes before slicing. With a sharp knife, cut the turkey roll into desired sized slices and serve.

Calories: 319 **Protein:** 50.1g **Carbs:** 4.2g **Fat:** 11.8g

Turkey Meatloaf

Serves: 4

Prep Time: 15 mins.

Cooking Time: 20 mins.

Ingredients:

- 455 grams ground turkey
- 52 grams onion, chopped
- 1 (113-grams) can chopped green chilies
- 1 egg, beaten
- 115 grams Monterey Jack cheese, grated
- 3 tablespoons fresh cilantro, chopped
- ½ teaspoon ground cumin
- Salt and ground black pepper, as required
- 55 grams fresh kale, trimmed and finely chopped
- 2 garlic cloves, minced
- 50 grams fresh breadcrumbs
- 65 grams salsa verde
- 1 teaspoon red chili powder
- ½ teaspoon dried oregano, crushed

Directions:

In a deep bowl, place all the ingredients and with your hands, mix until well combined. Divide the turkey mixture into 4 equal-sized portions and shape each into a mini loaf. Set the temperature of Air Fryer to 205 degrees C and preheat for 5 minutes. Arrange the loaves into the greased air fryer basket. Slide the basket in Air Fryer and set the time for 20 minutes. Remove from air fryer and place the loaves onto plates for about 5 minutes before serving. Serve warm.

Calories: 429 **Protein: 36.9g** **Carbs: 33.5g** **Fat: 18g**

Turkey Stuffed Capsicums

Serves: 4

Prep Time: 20 mins.

Cooking Time: 26 mins.

Ingredients:

- 1 teaspoon olive oil
- 2 garlic cloves, minced
- 1 teaspoon dried basil, crushed
- ½ teaspoon red chili powder
- 125 grams cooked jasmine rice
- 226 grams tomato sauce, divided
- 4 capsicums, tops removed and seeded
- ½ medium onion, chopped
- 455 grams ground turkey
- 1 teaspoon garlic salt
- Ground black pepper, as required
- 80 grams Mexican cheese, shredded and divided
- 2 teaspoons Worcestershire sauce

Directions:

In a medium-sized skillet, heat oil over medium heat and sauté the onion and garlic for about 3-5 minutes or until cooked thoroughly. Add the ground turkey, basil, and spices. Cook for about 8-10 minutes. Remove the skillet from heat and drain off the excess grease from skillet. Add the rice, half of the cheese, 2/3 of the tomato sauce and Worcestershire sauce and mix until well combined. Stuff each capsicum evenly with turkey mixture. Set the temperature of air fryer to 205 degrees C and preheat for 5 minutes. Arrange capsicums into the greased air fryer basket. Arrange the capsicums into the greased air fryer basket. Slide the basket in Air Fryer and set the time for 11 minutes. After 7 minutes of cooking, top each capsicum with the remaining tomato sauce, followed by the cheese. Serve warm.

Calories: 387 **Protein: 31.3g** **Carbs: 37.3g** **Fat: 13.7g**

Herbed Duck Legs

Serves: 2

Prep Time: 10 mins.

Cooking Time: 30 mins.

Ingredients:

- 1 garlic clove, minced
- ½ tablespoon fresh parsley, chopped
- Salt and ground black pepper, as required
- ½ tablespoon fresh thyme, chopped
- 1 teaspoon five-spice powder
- 2 duck legs

Directions:
In a bowl, mix together the garlic, herbs, five-spice powder, salt, and black pepper. Rub the duck legs with garlic mixture generously. Set the temperature of Air Fryer to 170 degrees C and preheat for 5 minutes. Arrange the duck legs into the greased air fryer basket. Slide the basket in Air Fryer and set the time for 25 minutes. After 25 minutes of cooking, set the temperature of Air fryer to 200 degrees C for 5 minutes. Serve hot.

Calories: 138   **Protein:** 25g   **Carbs:** 1g   **Fat:** 4.5g

Buttered Duck Breasts

Serves: 4

Prep Time: 10 mins.

Cooking Time: 22 mins.

Ingredients:

- 2 (340-grams) duck breasts
- 3 tablespoons unsalted butter, melted
- ¼ teaspoon star anise powder
- Salt and ground black pepper, as required
- ½ teaspoon dried thyme, crushed

Directions:
With a sharp knife, score the fat of duck breasts several times. Season the duck breasts generously with salt and black pepper. Set the temperature of Air Fryer to 200 degrees C and preheat for 5 minutes. Arrange the duck breasts into the greased air fryer basket. Slide the basket in Air Fryer and set the time for 22 minutes. After 10 minutes of cooking, coat the duck breasts with melted butter and sprinkle with thyme and star anise powder. Remove from Air Fryer and place the duck breasts onto a cutting board for about 5-10 minutes before slicing. With a sharp knife, cut each duck breast into desired sized slices and serve.

Calories: 296 **Protein:** 37.5g **Carbs:** 0.1g **Fat:** 15.5g

Red Meat Recipes

Buttered Rib-Eye Steak

Serves: 4

Prep Time: 15 mins.

Cooking Time: 14 mins.

Ingredients:

- 113 grams unsalted butter, softened
- 2 teaspoons garlic, minced
- Salt, as required
- Ground black pepper, as required
- 2 tablespoons fresh parsley, chopped
- 1 teaspoon Worcestershire sauce
- 2 (226-grams) rib-eye steaks
- 1 tablespoon olive oil

Directions:

In a bowl, add the butter, parsley, garlic, Worcestershire sauce, and salt and mix until well combined. Place the butter mixture onto parchment paper and roll into a log. Refrigerate until using. Coat the steak evenly with oil and then sprinkle with salt and black pepper. Set the temperature of Air Fryer to 205 degrees C and preheat for 5 minutes. Arrange the steaks into the greased air fryer basket. Slide the basket in Air Fryer and set the time for 14 minutes. Flip the steaks once halfway through. Remove from air fryer and place the steaks onto a platter for about 5 minutes. Cut each steak into desired sized slices and divide onto serving plates. Now, cut the butter log into slices. Top steak slices with butter slices and serve.

Calories: 459 **Protein:** 31.2g **Carbs:** 0.9g **Fat:** 36.5g

Bacon-Wrapped Filet Mignon

Serves: 2

Prep Time: 10 mins.

Cooking Time: 15 mins.

Ingredients:

- 2 bacon slices
- Salt and ground black pepper, as required
- 2 (150-grams) filet mignon steaks
- 1 teaspoon avocado oil

Directions:
Wrap 1 bacon slice around each mignon steak and secure with a toothpick. Season the steak evenly with salt and black pepper. Then, coat each steak with avocado oil. Set the temperature of Air Fryer to 190 degrees C and preheat for 5 minutes. Arrange the mignon steaks into the greased air fryer basket. Slide the basket in Air Fryer and set the time for 15 minutes. Flip the mignon steaks once halfway through. Serve hot.

Calories: 428 **Protein:** 52.9g **Carbs:** 0.5g **Fat:** 22.3g

Sweet & Sour Short Ribs

Serves: 8

Prep Time: 15 mins.

Cooking Time: 16 mins.

Ingredients:

- 1 kilogram 820 grams bone-in beef short ribs
- 1 tablespoon fresh ginger, finely grated
- 120 milliliters rice vinegar
- 2 tablespoons brown sugar
- 38 grams green onions, chopped
- 240 milliliters low-sodium soy sauce
- 1 tablespoon Sriracha
- 1 teaspoon ground black pepper

Directions:
In a resealable bag, put the ribs and all the above ingredients. Seal the bag and shake to coat well. Refrigerate overnight. Set the temperature of Air Fryer to 195 degrees C and preheat for 5 minutes. Arrange half of the ribs into the greased air fryer basket. Slide the basket in Air Fryer and set the time for 8 minutes. Flip the ribs once halfway through. Remove from air fryer and transfer onto a serving platter. Repeat with remaining ribs. Serve hot.

Calories: 502   **Protein:** 67.9g   **Carbs:** 5.6g   **Fat:** 20.6g

Parmesan Meatballs

Serves: 8

Prep Time: 20 mins.

Cooking Time: 17 mins.

Ingredients:

- 910 grams ground beef
- 27½ grams Parmigiana-Reggiano cheese, grated
- 4 tablespoons fresh parsley, chopped
- 1 teaspoon dried oregano, crushed
- 125 grams breadcrumbs
- 2 large eggs
- 1 small garlic clove, chopped
- Salt and ground black pepper, as required

Directions:
In a bowl, add all the ingredients and with your hands, mix until well combined. Gently shape the mixture into 5-centimeters balls. Set the temperature of Air Fryer to 175 degrees C and preheat for 5 minutes. Arrange the meatball into the air fryer basket in a single layer. Slide the basket in Air Fryer and set the time for 17 minutes. After 12 minutes of cooking, flip the meatballs once. Serve warm.

Calories: 307   **Protein: 36.9g**   **Carbs: 11.6g**   **Fat: 10.2g**

Beef Taco Wraps

Serves: 6

Prep Time: 15 mins.

Cooking Time: 4 mins.

Ingredients:

- 6 (30-centimeters) flour tortillas
- 340 grams nacho cheese
- 480 grams sour cream
- 3 Roma tomatoes, sliced
- Olive oil cooking spray
- 910 grams cooked ground beef
- 6 tostadas
- 150 grams Bibb lettuce, shredded
- 230 grams Mexican blend cheese, shredded

Directions:
Arrange the tortillas onto a smooth surface. Place the beef in the center of each tortilla evenly, followed by the nacho cheese, tostada, sour cream, lettuce, tomato slices and Mexican cheese. Bring the edges of each tortilla up, over the center to look like a pinwheel. Set the temperature of Air Fryer to 205 degrees C and preheat for 5 minutes. Arrange the taco wraps into the greased air fryer basket, seam side down and spray each with cooking spray. Slide the basket in Air Fryer and set the time for 4 minutes. After 2 minutes of cooking, flip the wraps and spray each with cooking spray again. Serve warm.

Calories: 960   **Protein: 68.4g**   **Carbs: 42.6g**   **Fat: 58.9g**

Glazed Pork Shoulder

Serves: 5

Prep Time: 15 mins.

Cooking Time: 18 mins.

Ingredients:

- 90 milliliters soy sauce
- 907 grams pork shoulder, cut into 3¾-centimeters thick slices
- 2 tablespoons sugar
- 1 tablespoon honey

Directions:
In a bowl, mix together the soy sauce, sugar, and honey. Add the pork and coat with marinade generously. Cover the bowl and refrigerate to marinate for about 4-6 hours. Set the temperature of Air Fryer to 180 degrees C and preheat for 5 minutes. Arrange the pork shoulder into the greased air fryer basket. Slide the basket in Air Fryer and set the time for 10 minutes. After 10 minutes of cooking, set the temperature of Air fryer to 200 degrees C for 8 minutes. Serve hot.

Calories: 507   **Protein:** 31.7g   **Carbs:** 9.7g   **Fat:** 36.9g

BBQ Pork Ribs

Serves: 4

Prep Time: 15 mins.

Cooking Time: 26 mins.

Ingredients:
- 75 grams honey, divided
- 2 tablespoons tomato ketchup
- 1 tablespoon soy sauce
- Ground white pepper, as required
- 169 grams BBQ sauce
- 1 tablespoon Worcestershire sauce
- ½ teaspoon garlic powder
- 795 grams pork ribs

Directions:
In a bowl, mix together 3 tablespoons of honey and the remaining ingredients except pork ribs. Add the pork ribs and coat with the mixture generously. Refrigerate to marinate for about 20 minutes. Set the temperature of Air Fryer to 180 degrees C and preheat for 5 minutes. Arrange the ribs into the greased air fryer basket. Slide the basket in Air Fryer and set the time for 26 minutes. Flip the ribs once halfway through. Remove from air fryer and transfer the ribs onto plates. Drizzle with the remaining honey and serve immediately.

Calories: 490   **Protein: 36g**   **Carbs: 34g**   **Fat: 23.2g**

Breaded Pork Chops

Serves: 2

Prep Time: 15 mins.

Cooking Time: 15 mins.

Ingredients:

- 2 (150-grams) pork chops
- 32½ grams plain flour
- 113 grams breadcrumbs
- Salt and ground black pepper, as required
- 1 egg
- 1 tablespoon vegetable oil

Directions:
Season each pork chop evenly with salt and pepper. In a shallow bowl, place the flour. In a second bowl, crack the egg and beat well. In a third bowl add the breadcrumbs and oil and mix until a crumbly mixture forms. Coat the pork chop with flour, then dip into beaten egg and finally, coat with the breadcrumb mixture. Set the temperature of Air Fryer to 205 degrees C and preheat for 5 minutes. Arrange the chops into the greased air fryer basket. Slide the basket in Air Fryer and set the time for 15 minutes. Flip the chops once halfway through. Serve hot.

Calories: 567 **Protein:** 38.8g **Carbs:** 54.7g **Fat:** 22g

Pork Rolls

Serves: 4

Prep Time: 15 mins.

Cooking Time: 15 mins.

Ingredients:

- 1 green onion, chopped
- 2 tablespoons fresh parsley, chopped
- 4 (150-grams) pork cutlets, pounded slightly
- ½ tablespoon olive oil
- 14 grams sun-dried tomatoes, finely chopped
- Salt and ground black pepper, as required
- 2 teaspoons paprika

Directions:
In a bowl, mix together the green onion, tomatoes, parsley, salt, and black pepper. Spread the tomato mixture over each pork cutlet. Roll each cutlet and secure with cocktail sticks. Rub the outer part of rolls with paprika, salt and black pepper. Coat the rolls with oil evenly. Set the temperature of Air Fryer to 200 degrees C and preheat for 5 minutes. Arrange the pork rolls into the greased air fryer basket. Slide the basket in Air Fryer and set the time for 15 minutes. Serve hot.

Calories: 206   **Protein: 33.5g**   **Carbs: 1.1g**   **Fat: 7.2g**

Glazed Ham

Serves: 4

Prep Time: 15 mins.

Cooking Time: 40 mins.

Ingredients:

- 752 grams ham
- 2 tablespoons French mustard
- 240 grams whiskey
- 2 tablespoons honey

Directions:
Place the ham at room temperature for about 30 minutes before cooking. In a bowl, mix together the whiskey, mustard, and honey. Place the ham in a baking dish that fits in the air fryer. Top with half of the honey mixture and coat well. Set the temperature of Air Fryer to 160 degrees C and preheat for 5 minutes. Arrange the baking dish into the air fryer basket. Slide the basket in Air Fryer and set the time for 40 minutes. After 15 minutes of cooking, flip the side of ham and top with the remaining honey mixture. Remove from air fryer and place the ham onto a platter for about 10 minutes before slicing. Cut the ham into desired size slices and serve.

Calories: 515   **Protein: 32.6g**   **Carbs: 17.9g**   **Fat: 17.8g**

Herbed Leg of Lamb

Serves: 5

Prep Time: 10 mins.

Cooking Time: 75 mins.

Ingredients:

- 907 grams bone-in leg of lamb
- Salt and ground black pepper, as required
- 2 fresh thyme sprigs
- 2 tablespoons olive oil
- 2 fresh rosemary sprigs

Directions:
Coat the leg of lamb with oil and sprinkle with salt and black pepper. Wrap the leg of lamb with herb sprigs. Set the temperature of Air Fryer to 150 degrees C and preheat for 5 minutes. Arrange the leg of lamb into the greased air fryer basket. Slide the basket in Air Fryer and set the time for 75 minutes. Remove from Air Fryer and transfer the leg of lamb onto a platter. With a piece of foil, cover the leg of lamb for about 10 minutes before slicing. Cut the leg of lamb into desired size pieces and serve.

Calories: 468   **Protein:** 32.2g   **Carbs:** 0.7g   **Fat:** 36.2g

Spiced Lamb Steaks

Serves: 3

Prep Time: 15 mins.

Cooking Time: 15 mins.

Ingredients:

- ½ of onion, roughly chopped
- 1 tablespoon fresh ginger, peeled
- 1 teaspoon ground fennel
- ½ teaspoon ground cinnamon
- Salt and ground black pepper, as required
- 5 garlic cloves, peeled
- 1 tablespoon fresh ginger, peeled
- ½ teaspoon ground cumin
- ½ teaspoon cayenne pepper
- 681 grams boneless lamb sirloin steaks

Directions:
In a blender, add the onion, garlic, ginger, and spices and pulse until smooth. Transfer the mixture into a large bowl. Add the lamb steaks and coat with the mixture generously. Refrigerate to marinate for about 24 hours. Set the temperature of Air Fryer to 165 degrees C and preheat for 5 minutes. Arrange the steaks into the greased air fryer basket in a single layer. Slide the basket in Air Fryer and set the time for 15 minutes. Flip the steaks once halfway through. Serve hot.

Calories: 368 **Protein:** 48.9g **Carbs:** 4.2g **Fat:** 17.9g

Pesto Rack of Lamb

Serves: 4

Prep Time: 16 mins.

Cooking Time: 15 mins.

Ingredients:

- ½ bunch fresh mint
- 60 milliliters extra-virgin olive oil
- Salt and ground black pepper, as required
- 1 garlic clove, peeled
- ½ tablespoon honey
- 1 (680-gramss) rack of lamb

Directions:
For pesto: in a blender, add the mint, garlic, oil, honey, salt, and black pepper and pulse until smooth. Coat the rack of lamb with pesto evenly. Set the temperature of Air Fryer to 95 degrees C and preheat for 5 minutes. Grease the Air Fryer basket. Place the rack of lamb into the prepared Air Fryer basket. Slide the basket into the Air Fryer and set the time for 15 minutes, coating with the remaining pesto after every 5 minutes. Remove from Air Fryer and place the rack of lamb onto a cutting board for about 5 minutes. Cut the rack into individual chops and serve.

Calories: 406 **Protein: 34.9g** **Carbs: 2.9g** **Fat: 27.7g**

Simple Lamb Chops

Serves: 2

Prep Time: 10 mins.

Cooking Time: 6 mins.

Ingredients:

- 1 tablespoon olive oil
- 4 (113-grams) lamb chops
- Salt and ground black pepper, as required

Directions:
In a large bowl, mix together the oil, salt, and black pepper. Add the chops and coat evenly with the mixture. Set the temperature of Air Fryer to 200 degrees C and preheat for 5 minutes. Arrange the chops into the greased air fryer basket. Slide the basket in Air Fryer and set the time for 6 minutes. Serve hot.

Calories: 486 **Protein: 63.8g** **Carbs: 0.8g** **Fat: 31.7g**

Mustard Lamb Chops

Serves: 2

Prep Time: 10 mins.

Cooking Time: 15 mins.

Ingredients:

- 1 tablespoon Dijon mustard
- ½ teaspoon olive oil
- Salt and ground black pepper, as required
- ½ tablespoon fresh lemon juice
- ½ teaspoon dried thyme
- 4 (113-grams) lamb loin chops

Directions:
In a large bowl, mix together the mustard, lemon juice, oil, tarragon, salt, and black pepper. Add chops and coat with the mixture generously. Set the temperature of Air Fryer to 200 degrees C and preheat for 5 minutes. Arrange chops into the greased air fryer basket in a single layer. Slide the basket in Air Fryer and set the time for 15 minutes. While cooking, flip the chops once halfway through. Serve hot.

Calories: 439   **Protein:** 64.1g   **Carbs:** 0.7g   **Fat:** 18.2g

Fish & Seafood Recipes

Spicy Salmon

Serves: 2

Prep Time: 10 mins.

Cooking Time: 11 mins.

Ingredients:

- 1 teaspoon smoked paprika
- 1 teaspoon onion powder
- Salt and ground black pepper, as required
- 2 teaspoons olive oil
- 1 teaspoon cayenne pepper
- 1 teaspoon garlic powder
- 2 (150-grams) (3¾-centimeters thick) salmon fillets

Directions:
In a bowl, add the spices and mix well. Drizzle the salmon fillets with oil and then, rub with the spice mixture. Set the temperature of Air Fryer to 200 degrees C and preheat for 5 minutes. Arrange the salmon fillets into the greased air fryer basket. Slide the basket in Air Fryer and set the time for 11 minutes. Serve hot.

Calories: 277   **Protein:** 33.5g   **Carbs:** 2.5g   **Fat:** 15.4g

Maple Salmon

Serves: 2

Prep Time: 10 mins.

Cooking Time: 8 mins.

Ingredients:

- 2 (150-grams) salmon fillets
- 2 tablespoons maple syrup
- Salt, as required

Directions:
Sprinkle the salmon fillets with salt and then, coat with maple syrup. Set the temperature of Air Fryer to 180 degrees C and preheat for 5 minutes. Arrange the salmon fillets into the greased air fryer basket. Slide the basket in Air Fryer and set the time for 8 minutes. Serve hot.

Calories: 277 **Protein:** 33g **Carbs:** 13.4g **Fat:** 10.5g

Cod Parcel

Serves: 4

Prep Time: 15 mins.

Cooking Time: 15 mins.

Ingredients:

- 2 tablespoons butter, melted
- ½ teaspoon dried tarragon
- 75 grams capsicums, seeded and thinly sliced
- 45 grams fennel bulbs, julienned
- 1 tablespoon olive oil
- 1 tablespoon fresh lemon juice
- Salt and ground black pepper, as required
- 45 grams carrots, peeled and julienned
- 2 (141-grams) frozen cod fillets, thawed

Directions:
In a large bowl, add butter, lemon juice, tarragon, salt, and black pepper and mix well. Add the capsicum, carrot, and fennel bulb and generously coat with the mixture. Arrange 2 large parchment squares onto a smooth surface. Coat the cod fillets with oil and then sprinkle with salt and black pepper. Arrange 1 cod fillet onto each parchment square and top each evenly with the vegetables. Top with any remaining sauce from the bowl. Fold the parchment paper and crimp the sides to secure fish and vegetables. Set the temperature of Air Fryer to 175 degrees C and preheat for 5 minutes. Arrange fish parcels into the Air fryer basket. Slide the basket in Air Fryer and set the time for 15 minutes. Remove from Air Fryer and place the parcels onto serving plates. Carefully open each parcel and serve warm.

Calories: 309   **Protein:** 26.6g   **Carbs:** 7.4g   **Fat:** 20.1g

Ranch Tilapia

Serves: 4

Prep Time: 10 mins.

Cooking Time: 13 mins.

Ingredients:

- 21 grams cornflakes, crushed
- 2½ tablespoons vegetable oil
- 2 eggs
- 1 (28-grams) packet dry ranch-style dressing mix
- 4 (150-grams) tilapia fillets

Directions:
In a shallow bowl, beat the eggs. In another bowl, add the cornflakes, ranch dressing, and oil and mix until a crumbly mixture forms. Dip the fish fillets into egg and then coat with the cornflake mixture. Set the temperature of Air Fryer to 180 degrees C and preheat for 5 minutes. Arrange the tilapia fillets into the greased air fryer basket. Slide the basket in Air Fryer and set the time for 13 minutes. Serve hot.

Calories: 274   **Protein: 31.1g**   **Carbs: 4.9g**   **Fat: 14.4g**

Glazed Halibut

Serves: 3

Prep Time: 15 mins.

Cooking Time: 15 mins.

Ingredients:
- 1 garlic clove, minced
- 120 milliliters cooking wine
- 60 milliliters fresh orange juice
- 50 grams sugar
- 455 grams halibut steak
- ¼ teaspoon fresh ginger, finely grated
- 120 milliliters low-sodium soy sauce
- 2 tablespoons lime juice
- ¼ teaspoon red pepper flakes, crushed

Directions:
In a medium pan, add garlic, ginger, wine, soy sauce, juices, sugar, and red pepper flakes and bring to a boil. Cook for about 3-4 minutes, stirring continuously. Remove the pan of the marinade from heat and let it cool. In a small bowl, add half of the marinade and reserve in a refrigerator. In a resealable bag, add the remaining marinade and halibut steak. Seal the bag and shake to coat well. Refrigerate for about 30 minutes. Set the temperature of Air Fryer to 200 degrees C and preheat for 5 minutes. Arrange the halibut steak into the air fryer basket. Slide the basket in Air Fryer and set the time for 11 minutes. Remove from air fryer and place the halibut steak onto a platter. Cut the steak into 3 equal-sized pieces and coat with the remaining glaze. Serve immediately.

Calories: 291   **Protein:** 34.9g   **Carbs:** 233   **Fat:** 3.6g

Sesame Seed Tuna

Serves: 2

Prep Time: 10 mins.

Cooking Time: 6 mins.

Ingredients:

- 1 egg white
- 1 tablespoon black sesame seeds
- 2 (150-grams) tuna steaks
- 32 grams white sesame seeds
- Salt and ground black pepper, as required

Directions:
In a shallow bowl, beat the egg white. In another bowl, mix together the sesame seeds, salt, and black pepper. Dip the tuna steaks into egg white and then coat with the sesame seeds mixture. Set the temperature of Air Fryer to 205 degrees C and preheat for 5 minutes. Arrange the tuna steaks into the greased air fryer basket. Slide the basket in Air Fryer and set the time for 6 minutes. Flip the tuna steaks once halfway through. Serve hot.

Calories: 425   **Protein: 55.9g**   **Carbs: 4.3g**   **Fat: 19.7g**

Shrimp Scampi

Serves: 4

Prep Time: 15 mins.

Cooking Time: 7 mins.

Ingredients:

- 4 tablespoons salted butter
- 1 tablespoon garlic, minced
- 455 grams shrimp, peeled and deveined
- 1 tablespoon fresh chives, chopped
- 1 tablespoon fresh lemon juice
- 2 teaspoons red pepper flakes, crushed
- 2 tablespoons fresh basil, chopped
- 2 tablespoons dry white wine

Directions:

Arrange a 17½-centimeters round baking pan into the air fryer basket. Slide the basket in Air Fryer and set the temperature of Air Fryer to 160 degrees C for about 8 minutes. Carefully remove the hot pan from air fryer basket. In the heated pan, place butter, lemon juice, garlic, and red pepper flakes and return the pan to Air fryer basket. Slide the basket in Air Fryer and set the time for 2 minutes. With a wooden spoon, stir the mixture once halfway through. Carefully remove the pan from Air fryer basket and stir in shrimp, basil, chives and wine. Return the pan to air fryer basket. Slide the basket in Air Fryer and set the time for 5 minutes. With a wooden spoon, stir the mixture once halfway through. Remove from Air Fryer and place the pan onto a wire rack for about 1 minute. Stir the mixture and transfer onto serving plates. Serve hot.

Calories: 780　　**Protein:** 81g　　**Carbs:** 3.3g　　**Fat:** 13.7g

Shrimp Kabobs

Serves: 2

Prep Time: 15 mins.

Cooking Time: 8 mins.

Ingredients:

- 340 grams shrimp, peeled and deveined
- 1 teaspoon garlic, minced
- ½ teaspoon ground cumin
- Salt and ground black pepper, as required
- 2 tablespoons fresh lemon juice
- ½ teaspoon paprika
- ½ teaspoon ground cumin
- 1 tablespoon fresh cilantro, chopped

Directions:
In a bowl, mix together the lemon juice, garlic, and spices. Add the shrimp and mix well. Thread the shrimp onto presoaked wooden skewers. Set the temperature of Air Fryer to 175 degrees C and preheat for 5 minutes. Arrange the shrimp skewers into the air fryer basket. Slide the basket in Air Fryer and set the time for 8 minutes. Flip the shrimp once halfway through. Remove from Air Fryer and transfer the shrimp kebabs onto serving plates. Garnish with fresh cilantro and serve immediately.

Calories: 212 **Protein:** 39.1g **Carbs:** 3.9g **Fat:** 3.2g

Prawn Burgers

Serves: 2

Prep Time: 20 mins.

Cooking Time: 6 mins.

Ingredients:

- 218 grams prawns, peeled, deveined and finely chopped
- ½ teaspoon fresh ginger, minced
- ½ teaspoon red chili powder
- Salt and ground black pepper, as required
- 50 grams breadcrumbs
- 2-3 tablespoons onion, finely chopped
- ½ teaspoon garlic, minced
- ½ teaspoon ground cumin

Directions:
In a large bowl, mix together the prawns, breadcrumbs, onion, ginger, garlic, and spices. Make small-sized patties from the mixture. Set the temperature of Air Fryer to 200 degrees C and preheat for 5 minutes. Arrange the patties into the greased air fryer basket in a single layer. Slide the basket in Air Fryer and set the time for 6 minutes. Serve warm.

Calories: 239 **Protein: 28.5g** **Carbs: 21.7g** **Fat: 3.5g**

Scallops with Spinach

Serves: 2

Prep Time: 15 mins.

Cooking Time: 10 mins.

Ingredients:

- 1 (340-grams) package frozen spinach, thawed and drained
- Salt and ground black pepper, as required
- 1 tablespoon tomato paste
- 1 tablespoon fresh basil, chopped
- 8 jumbo sea scallops
- Olive oil cooking spray
- 210 grams heavy whipping cream
- 1 teaspoon garlic, minced

Directions:
In the bottom of a 17½ centimeters heatproof pan, place the spinach. Spray each evenly with cooking spray and then sprinkle with a little salt and black pepper. Arrange scallops on top of the spinach in a single layer. In a bowl, mix well cream, tomato paste, garlic, basil, salt, and black pepper. Place the cream mixture evenly over the spinach and scallops. Set the temperature of Air Fryer to 175 degrees C and preheat for 5 minutes. Arrange the pan into the air fryer basket. Slide the basket in Air Fryer and set the time for 10 minutes. Serve hot.

Calories: 203   **Protein: 26.4g**   **Carbs: 12.3g**   **Fat: 18.3g**

Vegetarian Recipes

Hasselback Potatoes

Serves: 4

Prep Time: 15 mins.

Cooking Time: 30 mins.

Ingredients:

- 4 potatoes
- 2 tablespoons Parmesan cheese, shredded
- 2 tablespoons olive oil
- 1 tablespoon fresh chives, chopped

Directions:
With a sharp knife, cut slits along each potato the short way about 0.62-centimeters apart, making sure slices should stay connected at the bottom. Gently brush each potato with oil evenly. Set the temperature of Air Fryer to 180 degrees C and preheat for 5 minutes. Arrange the potatoes into the greased air fryer basket. Slide the basket in Air Fryer and set the time for 30 minutes. Coat the potatoes with the oil once halfway through. Remove from Air Fryer and transfer the potatoes onto a platter. Garnish with the cheeses and chives and serve immediately.

Calories: 218   **Protein:** 4.6g   **Carbs:** 33.6g   **Fat:** 7.9g

Parmesan Brussels Sprout

Serves: 3

Prep Time: 10 mins.

Cooking Time: 10 mins.

Ingredients:

- 455 grams Brussels sprouts, trimmed and halved
- Salt and ground black pepper, as required
- 27½ grams Parmesan cheese, shredded
- 1 tablespoon balsamic vinegar
- 1 tablespoon extra-virgin olive oil
- 25 grams whole-wheat breadcrumbs

Directions:
Set the temperature of Air Fryer to 205 degrees C and preheat for 5 minutes. In a bowl, mix together the Brussels sprouts, vinegar, oil, salt, and black pepper. Arrange Brussels sprouts into the greased air fryer basket in a single layer. Slide the basket in Air Fryer and set the time for 5 minutes. Remove from Air Fryer and flip the Brussels sprouts. Sprinkle the Brussels sprouts with breadcrumbs, followed by the cheese. Slide the basket in Air Fryer and set the time for 5 minutes. Serve hot.

Calories: 169   **Protein: 9.7g**   **Carbs: 20.2g**   **Fat: 7.6g**

Feta Spinach

Serves: 6

Prep Time: 15 mins.

Cooking Time: 6 mins.

Ingredients:

- 910 grams fresh spinach, chopped
- 1 jalapeño pepper, minced
- Salt and ground black pepper, as required
- 1 teaspoon fresh lemon zest, grated
- 1 garlic clove, minced
- 4 tablespoons butter, melted
- 110 grams feta cheese, crumbled

Directions:
In a bowl, add the spinach, garlic, jalapeño, butter, salt and black pepper and mix well. Set the temperature of Air Fryer to 170 degrees C and preheat for 5 minutes. Arrange the spinach mixture into the greased air fryer basket. Slide the basket in Air Fryer and set the time for 15 minutes. Remove from the air Fryer and transfer the spinach mixture into a bowl. Immediately stir in the cheese and lemon zest and serve hot.

Calories: 153   **Protein:** 7.1g   **Carbs:** 6.7g   **Fat:** 12.2g

Mushroom with Peas

Serves: 4

Prep Time: 10 mins.

Cooking Time: 15 mins.

Ingredients:

- 120 milliliters soy sauce
- 4 tablespoons rice vinegar
- 2 teaspoons Chinese five-spice powder
- 450 grams Cremini mushrooms, halved
- 4 tablespoons maple syrup
- 4 garlic cloves, finely chopped
- ½ teaspoon ground ginger
- 73 grams frozen peas

Directions:
In a bowl, add the soy sauce, maple syrup, vinegar, garlic, five-spice powder, and ground ginger and mix well. Set the temperature of Air Fryer to 175 degrees C and preheat for 5 minutes. Arrange the mushroom into the greased air fryer pan. Slide the pan in Air Fryer and set the time for 15 minutes. After 10 minutes of cooking, in the pan, add the peas and vinegar mixture and stir to combine. Serve hot.

Calories: 129 **Protein: 6g** **Carbs: 24.3g** **Fat: 0.2g**

Broccoli with Cauliflower

Serves: 2

Prep Time: 15 mins.

Cooking Time: 20 mins.

Ingredients:

- 135 grams broccoli, cut into 2½-centimeters pieces
- 1 tablespoon olive oil
- 160 grams cauliflower, cut into 2½-centimeters pieces
- Salt, as required

Directions:
In a bowl, add the vegetables, oil, and salt and toss to coat well. Set the temperature of Air Fryer to 190 degrees C and preheat for 5 minutes. Arrange the veggie mixture into the greased air fryer basket. Slide the basket in Air Fryer and set the time for 20 minutes. Toss the veggie mixture once halfway through. Serve hot.

Calories: 103 **Protein: 3.5g** **Carbs: 8.7g** **Fat: 7.3g**

Stuffed Tomatoes

Serves: 4

Prep Time: 15 mins.

Cooking Time: 22 mins.

Ingredients:

- 4 tomatoes
- 1 carrot, peeled and finely chopped
- 145 grams frozen peas, thawed
- 500 grams cold cooked rice
- 1 teaspoon olive oil
- 1 onion, chopped
- 1 garlic clove, minced
- 1 tablespoon soy sauce

Directions:

Cut the top of each tomato and scoop out pulp and seeds. In a skillet, heat oil over low heat and sauté the carrot, onion, garlic, and peas for about 2 minutes. Stir in the soy sauce and rice and remove from heat. Stuff each tomato with the rice mixture. Set the temperature of Air Fryer to 180 degrees C and preheat for 5 minutes. Arrange the tomatoes into the greased air fryer basket. Slide the basket in Air Fryer and set the time for 20 minutes. Remove from air fryer and transfer the tomatoes onto a serving platter. Set aside to cool slightly. Serve warm.

Calories: 421 **Protein: 10.5g** **Carbs: 89.1g** **Fat: 2.2g**

Oats & Beans Stuffed Capsicums

Serves: 2

Prep Time: 15 mins.

Cooking Time: 16 mins.

Ingredients:

- 2 large capsicums, halved lengthwise and seeded
- 4 tablespoons coconut yogurt
- ¼ teaspoon ground cumin
- Salt and ground black pepper, as required
- 468 grams cooked oatmeal
- 4 tablespoons canned red kidney beans, rinsed and drained
- ¼ teaspoon smoked paprika

Directions:
Set the temperature of Air Fryer to 180 degrees C and preheat for 5 minutes. Arrange the capsicums into the greased air fryer basket, cut-side down. Slide the basket in Air Fryer and set the time for 8 minutes. Remove from the air fryer and set the capsicums aside to cool. Meanwhile, in a bowl, add the oatmeal, beans, coconut yogurt, and spices and mix well. Stuff each capsicum half with the oatmeal mixture. Now, set the Air Fryer to 180 degrees C. Arrange capsicums into the air fryer basket. Slide the basket in Air Fryer and set the time for 8 minutes. Remove from air fryer and transfer the capsicums onto a serving platter. Set aside to cool slightly. Serve warm.

Calories: 453 **Protein:** 7.4g **Carbs:** 81g **Fat:** 19.1g

Tofu with Cauliflower

Serves: 2

Prep Time: 15 mins.

Cooking Time: 15 mins.

Ingredients:

- 1½ (1113-grams) block firm tofu, pressed and cubed
- 1 tablespoon nutritional yeast
- 1 teaspoon ground turmeric
- Salt and ground black pepper, as required
- ½ of small head cauliflower, cut into florets
- 1 tablespoon canola oil
- ¼ teaspoon dried parsley
- ¼ teaspoon paprika

Directions:
In a bowl, add all the ingredients and mix well. Set the temperature of Air Fryer to 200 degrees C and preheat for 5 minutes. Arrange the tofu mixture into the greased air fryer basket. Slide the basket in Air Fryer and set the time for 15 minutes. Shake the basket once halfway through. Serve hot.

Calories: 170 **Protein:** 11.6g **Carbs:** 8.3g **Fat:** 11.9g

Beans & Veggie Burgers

Serves: 4

Prep Time: 20 mins.

Cooking Time: 22 mins.

Ingredients:

- 172 grams cooked black bean
- 30 grams fresh spinach, chopped
- 2 teaspoons Chile lime seasoning
- 330 grams boiled potatoes, peeled and mashed
- 100 grams fresh mushrooms, chopped
- Olive oil cooking spray

Directions:
In a large bowl, add the beans, potatoes, spinach, mushrooms, and seasoning and with your hands, mix until well combined. Make 4 equal-sized patties from the mixture. Set the temperature of Air Fryer to 190 degrees C and preheat for 5 minutes. Arrange the patties into the air fryer basket. Slide the basket in Air Fryer and set the time for 19 minutes. After 12 minutes of cooking, flip the patties. After 19 minutes of cooking, set the temperature of Air Fryer to 32 degrees C for 3 more minutes. Serve warm.

Calories: 121   **Protein: 26.2g**   **Carbs: 24.3g**   **Fat: 0.4g**

Veggie Rice

Serves: 3

Prep Time: 15 mins.

Cooking Time: 18 mins.

Ingredients:

- 500 grams cooked white rice
- 2 teaspoons sesame oil, toasted and divided
- Salt and ground white pepper, as required
- 73 grams frozen peas, thawed
- 1 teaspoon low-sodium soy sauce
- ½ teaspoon sesame seeds, toasted
- 1 tablespoon vegetable oil
- 1 tablespoon water
- 1 large egg, lightly beaten
- 45 grams frozen carrots, thawed
- 1 teaspoon Sriracha sauce

Directions:
In a large bowl, add the rice, vegetable oil, one teaspoon of sesame oil, water, salt, and white pepper and mix well. Set the temperature of Air Fryer to 195 degrees C and preheat for 5 minutes. Place the rice mixture into the greased air fryer pan. Slide the pan in Air Fryer and set the time for 18 minutes. After 6 minutes of cooking, stir the rice mixture. After 12 minutes of cooking, place the beaten egg over rice mixture. After 16 minutes of cooking, stir in the peas and carrots. Meanwhile, in a bowl, mix together soy sauce, Sriracha sauce, sesame seeds and the remaining sesame oil. Remove from Air Fryer and transfer the rice mixture into a serving bowl. Drizzle with the sauce and serve.

Calories: 350 **Protein:** 8.1g **Carbs:** 54.7g **Fat:** 10g

Snacks Recipes

Roasted Cashews

Serves: 8

Prep Time: 10 mins.

Cooking Time: 4 mins.

Ingredients:

- 260 grams raw cashew nuts
- Salt and ground black pepper, as required
- 1 teaspoon butter, melted

Directions:
In a bowl, mix together all the ingredients. Set the temperature of Air Fryer to 180 degrees C and preheat for 5 minutes. Arrange the cashews into the greased air fryer basket in a single layer. Slide the basket in Air Fryer and set the time for 4 minutes. Shake the cashews once halfway through. Remove from the Air Fryer and transfer the hot nuts in a glass bowl and serve.

Calories: 201   **Protein: 5.3g**   **Carbs: 11.2g**   **Fat: 16.4g**

Apple Chips

Serves: 2

Prep Time: 10 mins.

Cooking Time: 16 mins.

Ingredients:

- 1 apple, peeled, cored and thinly sliced
- ½ teaspoon ground cinnamon
- Pinch of ground ginger
- 1 tablespoon sugar
- Pinch of ground cardamom
- Pinch of salt

Directions:
In a bowl, add all the ingredients and toss to coat well. Set the temperature of Air Fryer to 200 degrees C and preheat for 5 minutes. Arrange the apple slices into the air fryer basket in a single layer in 2 batches. Slide the basket in Air Fryer and set the time for 8 minutes. Flip the apple slices once halfway through.

Calories: 72   **Protein: 0.3g**   **Carbs: 19.2g**   **Fat: 0.2g**

French Fries

Serves: 8

Prep Time: 15 mins.

Cooking Time: 30 mins.

Ingredients:

- 795 grams potatoes, peeled and cut into strips
- 1 teaspoon onion powder
- 60 milliliters olive oil
- 2 teaspoons paprika

Directions:

In a large bowl, add the water and potato strips. Set aside for about 1 hour. Drain the potato strips well and pat them dry with paper towels. In a large bowl, add the potato strips and the remaining ingredients and toss to coat well. Set the temperature of Air Fryer to 190 degrees C and preheat for 5 minutes. Arrange the potato strips into the air fryer basket in a single layer. Slide the basket in Air Fryer and set the time for 30 minutes. Serve warm.

Calories: 132   **Protein: 1.8g**   **Carbs: 16.2g**   **Fat: 7.3g**

Onion Rings

Serves: 4

Prep Time: 20 mins.

Cooking Time: 10 mins.

Ingredients:

- 1 large onion, cut into 0.60-centimeters slices
- 1 teaspoon baking powder
- 240 milliliters milk
- 75 grams dry breadcrumbs
- 160 grams all-purpose flour
- Salt, as required
- 1 egg

Directions:
Separate the onion slices into rings. In a shallow dish, mix together the flour, baking powder, and salt. In a second dish, add the milk and egg and beat well. In a third dish, place the breadcrumbs. Coat each onion ring with flour mixture, then dip into egg mixture and finally, coat evenly with the breadcrumbs. Set the temperature of Air Fryer to 185 degrees C and preheat for 5 minutes. Arrange the onion rings into the air fryer basket in a single layer. Slide the basket in Air Fryer and set the time for 10 minutes. Serve hot.

Calories: 285   **Protein: 10.5g**   **Carbs: 51.6g**   **Fat: 3.8g**

Mozzarella Sticks

Serves: 4

Prep Time: 15 mins.

Cooking Time: 24 mins.

Ingredients:

- 32½ grams white flour
- 3 tablespoons non-fat milk
- 455 grams Mozzarella cheese block cut into 7½x1¼-centimeters sticks
- 2 eggs
- 100 grams plain breadcrumbs

Directions:
In a shallow dish, place the flour. In a second dish, mix together the eggs, and milk. In a third dish, place the breadcrumbs. Coat the Mozzarella sticks with flour, then dip into egg mixture and finally, coat evenly with the breadcrumbs. Arrange the Mozzarella sticks onto a baking sheet and freeze for about 1-2 hours. Set the temperature of Air Fryer to 225 degrees C and preheat for 5 minutes. Arrange the Mozzarella sticks into the lightly greased air fryer basket in a single layer in 2 batches. Slide the basket in Air Fryer and set the time for 12 minutes. Serve warm.

Calories: 255   **Protein: 16.4g**   **Carbs: 26.1g**   **Fat: 9.3g**

Broccoli Poppers

Serves: 4

Prep Time: 15 mins.

Cooking Time: 10 mins.

Ingredients:

- 2 tablespoons plain yogurt
- ¼ teaspoon ground cumin
- Salt, as required
- 2 tablespoons chickpea flour
- ½ teaspoon red chili powder
- ¼ teaspoon ground turmeric
- 455 grams broccoli, cut into small florets

Directions:

In a bowl, mix together the yogurt and spices. Add the broccoli and coat with marinade generously. Refrigerate for about 20 minutes. Remove from the refrigerator and sprinkle the broccoli florets with chickpea flour. Set the temperature of Air Fryer to 205 degrees C and preheat for 5 minutes. Arrange the broccoli florets into the greased air fryer basket. Slide the basket in Air Fryer and set the time for 10 minutes. Toss the broccoli florets once halfway through. Serve hot.

Calories: 69   **Protein: 4.9g**   **Carbs: 12.2g**   **Fat: 0.9g**

Chicken Nuggets

Serves: 4

Prep Time: 15 mins.

Cooking Time: 10 mins.

Ingredients:

- ½ of courgette, roughly chopped
- 396 grams boneless, skinless chicken breast, cut into chunks
- 1 tablespoon onion powder
- 130 grams all-purpose flour
- 1 egg
- ½ of carrot, roughly chopped
- ½ tablespoon mustard powder
- 1 tablespoon garlic powder
- Salt and ground black pepper, as required
- 2 tablespoons milk
- 100 grams panko breadcrumbs

Directions:
In a food processor, add the courgette and carrot and pulse until finely chopped. Add the chicken, mustard powder, garlic powder, onion powder, salt, and black pepper and pulse until well combined. In a shallow dish, place the flour. In a second dish, mix together the milk, and egg. In a third dish, place the breadcrumbs. Coat the nuggets with flour, then dip into egg mixture and finally, coat with the breadcrumbs. Set the temperature of Air Fryer to 200 degrees C and preheat for 5 minutes. Arrange the cake pan into the greased air fryer basket. Slide the basket in Air Fryer and set the time for 10 minutes. Serve hot.

Calories: 375 **Protein: 28g** **Carbs: 34.4g** **Fat: 6.4g**

Buffalo Chicken Wings

Serves: 6

Prep Time: 15 mins.

Cooking Time: 22 mins.

Ingredients:

- 910 grams chicken wings, cut into drumettes and flats
- Ground black pepper, as required
- 78 grams red hot sauce
- 1 teaspoon chicken seasoning
- 1 teaspoon garlic powder
- 1 tablespoon olive oil
- 2 tablespoons low-sodium soy sauce

Directions:

Sprinkle each chicken wing with chicken seasoning, garlic powder, and black pepper evenly. Set the temperature of Air Fryer to 205 degrees C and preheat for 5 minutes. Arrange the chicken wings into the greased air fryer basket. Slide the basket in Air Fryer and set the time for 10 minutes. Shake the basket once halfway through. Remove from Air Fryer and transfer the chicken wings into a bowl. Drizzle with the red hot sauce, oil, and soy sauce and toss to coat well.

Again, arrange the chicken wings into the air fryer basket in a single layer and slide in Air Fryer. Set the temperature of Air Fryer to 205 degrees C for 12 minutes. Serve hot.

Calories: 313 **Protein:** 44.6g **Carbs:** 0.9g **Fat:** 13.6g

Bacon-Wrapped Shrimp

Serves: 6

Prep Time: 15 mins.

Cooking Time: 7 mins.

Ingredients:

- ❖ 455 grams shrimp, peeled and deveined
- ❖ 455 grams bacon, thinly sliced

Directions:
Wrap each shrimp with one bacon slice. Place the shrimp into a baking dish and refrigerate for about 20 minutes. Set the temperature of Air Fryer to 200 degrees C and preheat for 5 minutes. Arrange the shrimp into the air fryer basket. Slide the basket in Air Fryer and set the time for 7 minutes. Serve warm.

Calories: 458   **Protein: 40.3g**   **Carbs: 1.1g**   **Fat: 31.7g**

Crispy Prawns

Serves: 4

Prep Time: 15 mins.

Cooking Time: 8 mins.

Ingredients:

- ❖ 1 egg
- ❖ 18 prawns, peeled and deveined
- ❖ 226 grams nacho chips, crushed

Directions:
In a shallow dish, crack the egg, and beat well. In another dish, place the crushed nacho chips. Dip the prawn into beaten egg and then coat with the nacho chips. Set the temperature of Air Fryer to 180 degrees C and preheat for 5 minutes. Arrange the prawns into the greased air fryer basket. Slide the basket in Air Fryer and set the time for 8 minutes. Serve hot.

Calories: 425   **Protein: 28.6g**   **Carbs: 36.6g**   **Fat: 17.6g**

Dessert Recipes

Stuffed Apples

Serves: 4

Prep Time: 15 mins.

Cooking Time: 13 mins.

Ingredients:

For Stuffed Apples

- 4 small firm apples, cored
- 75 grams golden raisins
- 70 grams blanched almonds
- 2 tablespoons sugar

For Vanilla Sauce

- 120 grams whipped cream
- 2 tablespoons sugar
- ½ teaspoon vanilla extract

Directions:
In a food processor, add raisins, almonds, and sugar and pulse until chopped. Carefully, stuff each apple with raisin mixture. Line a baking dish with parchment paper. Arrange the apples into the prepared baking dish. Set the temperature of Air Fryer to 180 degrees C and preheat for 5 minutes. Arrange the baking dish into the air fryer basket. Slide the basket in Air Fryer and set the time for 10 minutes. Meanwhile, for vanilla sauce: in a pan, add the cream, sugar, and vanilla extract over medium heat and cook for about 2-3 minutes or until sugar is dissolved, stirring continuously. Remove the baking dish from Air Fryer and transfer the apples onto plates to cool slightly. Top with the vanilla sauce and serve.

Calories: 378 **Protein: 5.4g** **Carbs: 54.7g** **Fat: 18.4g**

Brownie Muffins

Serves: 12

Prep Time: 10 mins.

Cooking Time: 10 mins.

Ingredients:

- 1 package Betty Crocker fudge brownie mix
- 1 egg
- 2 teaspoons water
- 25 grams walnuts, chopped
- 90 milliliters vegetable oil

Directions:
In a bowl, add all the ingredients and mix well. Place mixture into 12 greased muffin molds. Set the temperature of Air Fryer to 150 degrees C and preheat for 5 minutes. Arrange the muffin molds into the air fryer basket. Slide the basket in Air Fryer and set the time for 10 minutes. Remove the muffin molds from Air Fryer and place onto a wire rack to cool for about 10 minutes. Carefully invert the muffins onto wire rack to completely cool before serving.

Calories: 241   **Protein:** 2.8g   **Carbs:** 36.9g   **Fat:** 9.6g

Shortbread Fingers

Serves: 10

Prep Time: 15 mins.

Cooking Time: 12 mins.

Ingredients:

- ❖ 75 grams caster sugar
- ❖ 170 grams butter
- ❖ 19 grams plus 2½ tablespoons plain flour

Directions:
In a large bowl, mix together the sugar and flour. Add the butter and mix until a smooth dough forms. Cut the dough into 10 equal-sized fingers. With a fork, lightly prick the fingers. Arrange fingers onto the greased baking sheet in a single layer. Set the temperature of Air Fryer to 175 degrees C and preheat for 5 minutes. Arrange the baking sheet into the air fryer basket. Slide the basket in Air Fryer and set the time for 12 minutes. Remove the baking sheet from Air Fryer and place onto a wire rack to cool for about 5-10 minutes. Now, invert the shortbread fingers onto the wire rack to completely cool before serving.

Calories: 224 **Protein:** 2.3g **Carbs:** 22.6g **Fat:** 15g

Lava Cake

Serves: 4

Prep Time: 10 mins.

Cooking Time: 12½ mins.

Ingredients:

- 115 grams chocolate chips
- 2 large eggs
- 130 grams confectioners 'sugar
- 11¼ grams all-purpose flour
- 47 grams fresh raspberries
- 113 grams unsalted butter, softened
- 2 large egg yolks
- 1 teaspoon peppermint extract
- 2 tablespoons powdered sugar

Directions:

In a microwave-safe bowl, put the chocolate chips and butter. Microwave on high heat for about 30 seconds. Remove the bowl from microwave and stir the mixture well. Add the eggs, egg yolks and confectioners' sugar and whisk until well combined. Add the flour and gently stir. Grease 4 ramekins and dust each with a little flour. Place mixture into the prepared ramekins evenly. Set the temperature of Air Fryer to 190 degrees C and preheat for 5 minutes. Arrange the ramekins into the air fryer basket. Slide the basket in Air Fryer and set the time for 12 minutes. Remove from air fryer and place the ramekins onto a wire rack for about 5 minutes. Carefully run a knife around the sides of each ramekin several times to loosen the cake. Now invert each cake onto a dessert plate and dust with powdered sugar. Garnish with raspberries and serve immediately.

Calories: 516   **Protein: 5.2g**   **Carbs: 51.7g**   **Fat: 32.2g**

Butter Cake

Serves: 6

Prep Time: 15 mins.

Cooking Time: 15 mins.

Ingredients:

- ❖ 85 grams butter, softened
- ❖ 1 egg
- ❖ Pinch of salt
- ❖ 1 tablespoon icing sugar
- ❖ 100 grams caster sugar
- ❖ 179 grams plain flour, sifted
- ❖ 120 milliliters milk

Directions:
In a bowl, add the butter and sugar and beat until light and creamy. Add in the egg and beat until smooth and fluffy. Now, add the flour and salt and mix well alternately with the milk. Place mixture evenly into the greased Bundt cake pan. Set the temperature of Air Fryer to 175 degrees C and preheat for 5 minutes. Arrange the cake pan into the air fryer basket. Slide the basket in Air Fryer and set the time for 15 minutes. Remove the cake pan from Air Fryer and place onto a wire rack to cool for about 10 minutes. Now, invert the cake onto wire rack to completely cool before slicing. Dust the cake with icing sugar and cut into desired sized slices before serving.

Calories: 299 **Protein:** 4.8g **Carbs:** 41.8g **Fat:** 12.9g

Simple Cheesecake

Serves: 2

Prep Time: 10 mins.

Cooking Time: 10 mins.

Ingredients:

- 150 grams Erythritol
- 1 teaspoon vanilla extract
- 450 grams cream cheese, softened
- 2 eggs
- ½ teaspoon fresh lemon juice
- 2 tablespoon sour cream

Directions:
In a blender, add the Erythritol, eggs, vanilla extract and lemon juice and pulse until smooth. Add the cream cheese and sour cream and pulse until smooth. Place the mixture into 2 (10-centimeters) springform pans evenly. Set the temperature of Air Fryer to 175 degrees C and preheat for 5 minutes. Arrange the springform pans into the air fryer basket. Slide the basket in Air Fryer and set the time for 10 minutes. Remove from the Air Fryer and place the pans onto a wire rack to cool. Refrigerate overnight before serving.

Calories: 886　　**Protein: 23.1g**　　**Carbs: 7.2g**　　**Fat: 86g**

Cherry Clafoutis

Serves: 4

Prep Time: 15 mins.

Cooking Time: 25 mins.

Ingredients:

- 332 grams fresh cherries, pitted
- 32½ grams flour
- Pinch of salt
- 1 egg
- 33 grams powdered sugar
- 3 tablespoons vodka
- 2 tablespoons sugar
- 120 grams sour cream
- 1 tablespoon butter

Directions:
In a bowl, mix together the cherries and vodka. In another bowl, add the flour, sugar, and salt and mix well. Add the sour cream, and egg and mix until a smooth dough forms. Place flour mixture evenly into a greased cake pan. Spread cherry mixture over the dough. Place butter on top in the form of dots. Set the temperature of Air Fryer to 180 degrees C and preheat for 5 minutes. Arrange the cake pan into the air fryer basket. Slide the basket in Air Fryer and set the time for 25 minutes. Remove the cake pan from air fryer and place onto a wire rack to cool for about 10 minutes. Now, invert the Clafoutis onto a platter and sprinkle with powdered sugar. Cut the Clafoutis into desired size slices and serve warm.

Calories: 309 **Protein:** 3.5g **Carbs:** 45g **Fat:** 10.4g

Apple Crumble

Serves: 4

Prep Time: 10 mins.

Cooking Time: 25 mins.

Ingredients:

- 1 can apple pie filling
- 9 tablespoons self-rising flour
- Pinch of salt
- 60 grams butter, softened
- 7 tablespoons caster sugar

Directions:
Place apple pie filling evenly into a lightly greased prepared baking dish. In a medium bowl, add the remaining ingredients and mix until a crumbly mixture forms. Spread the mixture over apple pie filling evenly. Set the temperature of Air Fryer to 160 degrees C and preheat for 5 minutes. Arrange the baking dish into the air fryer basket. Slide the basket in Air Fryer and set the time for 25 minutes. Remove the baking dish from air fryer and place onto a wire rack to cool for about 10 minutes. Serve warm.

Calories: 340   **Protein: 2g**   **Carbs: 60.3g**   **Fat: 11.8g**

Fudge Brownies

Serves: 8

Prep Time: 15 mins.

Cooking Time: 20 mins.

Ingredients:

- 200 grams sugar
- 65 grams flour
- 1 teaspoon baking powder
- 1 teaspoon vanilla extract
- 113 grams butter, melted
- 45 grams cocoa powder
- 2 eggs

Directions:
In a large bowl, add the sugar, and butter and whisk until light and fluffy. Add the remaining ingredients and mix until well combined. Place mixture into a greased baking pan and with the back of a spatula, smooth the top surface. Set the temperature of Air Fryer to 175 degrees C and preheat for 5 minutes. Arrange the baking pan into the air fryer basket. Slide the basket in Air Fryer and set the time for 20 minutes. Remove the baking pan from air fryer and set aside to cool completely. Cut into 8 equal-sized squares and serve.

Calories: 255 **Protein:** 3.8g **Carbs:** 34.8g **Fat:** 13.4g

Raisin Bread Pudding

Serves: 3

Prep Time: 15 mins.

Cooking Time: 12 mins.

Ingredients:

- 240 milliliters milk
- 1 tablespoon brown sugar
- ¼ teaspoon vanilla extract
- 2 bread slices, cut into small cubes
- 1 tablespoon chocolate chips
- 1 egg
- ½ teaspoon ground cinnamon
- 2 tablespoons raisins, soaked in hot water for about 15 minutes
- 1 tablespoon sugar

Directions:
In a bowl, add the milk, egg, brown sugar, cinnamon, and vanilla extract and mix well. Stir in the raisins. In a baking dish, spread the bread cubes and top with the milk mixture evenly. Refrigerate for about 15-20 minutes. Set the temperature of Air Fryer to 190 degrees C and preheat for 5 minutes. Remove the baking dish from refrigerator and sprinkle with chocolate chips and sugar on top. Arrange the baking dish into the air fryer basket. Slide the basket in Air Fryer and set the time for 12 minutes. Serve warm.

Calories: 143   **Protein: 5.5g**   **Carbs: 21.3g**   **Fat: 4.4g**

Keto Air Fryer Recipes

Parsley Soufflé

Serves: 2

Prep Time: 10 mins.

Cooking Time: 8 mins.

Ingredients:

- 2 tablespoons light cream
- 1 tablespoon fresh parsley, chopped
- Salt, as required
- 2 large organic eggs
- 1 jalapeño pepper, chopped

Directions:
Grease 2 soufflé dishes. In a bowl, add all ingredients and beat until well combined. Divide the mixture into the prepared soufflé dishes evenly. Set the temperature of Air Fryer to 200 degrees C and preheat for 5 minutes. Arrange the soufflé dishes into the air fryer basket. Slide the basket in Air Fryer and set the time for 8 minutes. Serve hot.

Calories: 118   **Protein:** 6.8g   **Carbs:** 1.4g   **Fat:** 9.7g

Ham Casserole

Serves: 2

Prep Time: 10 mins.

Cooking Time: 15 mins.

Ingredients:

- 4 large organic eggs, divided
- 2 tablespoons heavy cream
- 56 grams ham, sliced thinly
- 3 tablespoons Parmesan cheese, grated
- Salt and ground black pepper, as required
- 2 teaspoons unsalted butter, softened
- 1/8 teaspoon smoked paprika
- 2 teaspoon fresh chives, minced

Directions:
In a bowl, add 1 egg, salt, black pepper and cream and beat until smooth. In the bottom of a pie dish, spread the butter. Place the ham slices over the butter and top with the egg mixture evenly. Carefully crack the remaining eggs on top and sprinkle with paprika, salt and black pepper. Top with cheese and chives evenly. Set the temperature of Air Fryer to 160 degrees C and preheat for 5 minutes. Arrange the pie dish into the air fryer basket. Slide the basket in Air Fryer and set the time for 12 minutes. Remove the pie dish from Air Fryer and place onto a wire rack to cool for about 5 minutes before serving.

Calories: 302 **Protein: 20.7g** **Carbs: 2.4g** **Fat: 20.7g**

Pumpkin Bread

Serves: 4

Prep Time: 15 mins.

Cooking Time: 25 mins.

Ingredients:

- 22 grams coconut flour
- 1 teaspoon organic baking powder
- ¼ teaspoon ground cinnamon
- 4 tablespoons sugar-free canned pumpkin
- 2 tablespoons unsweetened almond milk
- 2 tablespoons stevia blend
- ¾ teaspoon pumpkin pie spice
- 1/8 teaspoon salt
- 2 large organic eggs
- 1 teaspoon organic vanilla extract

Directions:
In a bowl, mix together the flour, stevia, baking powder, spices, and salt. In another large bowl, add the pumpkin, eggs, almond milk, and vanilla extract. Beat until well combined. Then, add in the flour mixture and mix until just combined. Line a cake pan with a greased parchment paper. Place the mixture into the prepared pan. Set the temperature of Air Fryer to 175 degrees C and preheat for 5 minutes. Place the mixture into a greased loaf pan. Arrange the pan into the air fryer basket. Slide the basket in Air Fryer and set the time for 25 minutes. Remove from Air Fryer and place the pan onto a wire rack for about 10-15 minutes. Carefully invert the bread onto the wire rack to cool completely cool before slicing. Cut the bread into desired sized slices and serve.

Calories: 78   **Protein: 4.4g**   **Carbs: 7g**   **Fat: 3.4g**

2-Ingredients Chicken Breasts

Serves: 4

Prep Time: 10 mins.

Cooking Time: 21 mins.

Ingredients:

- ❖ 4 (150-grams) grass-fed boneless, skinless chicken breasts
- ❖ 150 grams Italian salad dressing

Directions:
In a large bowl, add the chicken breasts and dressing and mix well. Cover the bowl and refrigerate overnight. Set the temperature of Air Fryer to 190 degrees C and preheat for 5 minutes. Arrange the chicken breasts into the greased air fryer basket. Slide the basket in Air Fryer and set the time for 21 minutes. While cooking, flip the chicken breasts twice after every 7 minutes. Serve hot.

Calories: 595   **Protein: 43.5g**   **Carbs: 3.9g**   **Fat: 21.8g**

Parmesan Chicken Thighs

Serves: 4

Prep Time: 15 mins.

Cooking Time: 18 mins.

Ingredients:

- 4 (150-grams) grass-fed bone-in, skin-on chicken thighs
- ½ teaspoon Italian seasoning
- Olive oil cooking spray
- 2 tablespoons Parmesan cheese, grated
- 2 garlic cloves, mashed into a paste
- Salt and ground black pepper, as required

Directions:
Season the chicken thighs with salt and black pepper. Place the chicken thighs onto a plate, skin-side up and sprinkle with Parmesan, followed by garlic and Italian seasoning. Set the temperature of Air Fryer to 195 degrees C and preheat for 5 minutes. Arrange the chicken thighs into the greased air fryer basket and spray with cooking spray. Slide the basket in Air Fryer and set the time for 18 minutes. After 12 minutes of cooking, flip the chicken thighs. Serve hot.

Calories: 336   **Protein: 50.3g**   **Carbs: 0.6g**   **Fat: 13.4g**

Stuffed Chicken Breasts

Serves: 2

Prep Time: 15 mins.

Cooking Time: 30 mins.

Ingredients:

- 1 tablespoon olive oil
- 60 grams ricotta cheese, shredded
- Salt and ground black pepper, as required
- 2 tablespoons Parmesan cheese, grated
- 50 grams fresh spinach
- 2 (113-grams) grass-fed skinless, boneless chicken breasts
- ¼ teaspoon paprika

Directions:

In a medium skillet, heat the oil over medium heat and cook the spinach for about 3-4 minutes. Stir in the ricotta and cook for about 40-60 seconds. Remove the skillet from heat and set aside to cool. Cut slits into the chicken breasts about 0.62-centimeters apart but not all the way through. Stuff each chicken breast with the spinach mixture. Season each chicken breast with salt and black pepper and then sprinkle the top with Parmesan cheese and paprika. Set the temperature of Air Fryer to 200 degrees C and preheat for 5 minutes. Arrange the chicken breasts into the greased air fryer basket in a single layer. Slide the basket in Air Fryer and set the time for 20-25 minutes. Serve hot.

Calories: 269   **Protein: 32.8g**   **Carbs: 2.7g**   **Fat: 14.9g**

Turkey Feta Burgers

Serves: 2

Prep Time: 15 mins.

Cooking Time: 15 mins.

Ingredients:

- 226 grams ground turkey breast
- 2 garlic cloves, grated
- ½ teaspoons red pepper flakes, crushed
- 27½ grams feta cheese, crumbled
- 1½ tablespoons olive oil
- 2 teaspoons fresh oregano, chopped
- Salt, as required

Directions:
In a large bowl, add all the ingredients except for cheese and mix until well combined. Make 2 (1¼-centimeters thick) patties from the mixture. Set the temperature of Air Fryer to 185 degrees C and preheat for 5 minutes. Arrange the patties into the greased air fryer basket. Slide the basket in Air Fryer and set the time for 15 minutes. While cooking, flip the patties once halfway through. Serve hot with the topping of feta.

Calories: 279 **Protein:** 25g **Carbs:** 2.8g **Fat:** 19.3g

Buttered Fillet Mignon

Serves: 4

Prep Time: 10 mins.

Cooking Time: 14 mins.

Ingredients:

- 2 (150-grams) grass-fed filet mignon steaks
- Salt and ground black pepper, as required
- 1 tablespoon butter, softened

Directions:
Coat each steak with butter and then season with salt and black pepper. Set the temperature of Air Fryer to 200 degrees C and preheat for 5 minutes. Arrange the steaks into the greased air fryer basket. Slide the basket in Air Fryer and set the time for 14 minutes. Flip the steaks once halfway through. Serve hot.

Calories: 362 **Protein:** 42.9g **Carbs:** 0g **Fat:** 20g

Herbed Beef Roast

Serves: 5

Prep Time: 10 mins.

Cooking Time: 45 mins.

Ingredients:

- 910 grams grass-fed beef roast
- 1 teaspoon dried rosemary, crushed
- Salt, as required
- 1 tablespoon olive oil
- 1 teaspoon dried thyme, crushed

Directions:

In a bowl, mix together the oil, herbs, and salt. Coat the roast with herb mixture evenly. Set the temperature of Air Fryer to 185 degrees C and preheat for 5 minutes. Arrange the roast into the greased air fryer basket. Slide the basket in Air Fryer and set the time for 45 minutes. Remove from Air Fryer and transfer the roast onto a platter. With a piece of foil, cover the roast for about 10 minutes before slicing. Cut the roast into desired size slices and serve.

Calories: 363　　**Protein:** 55.1g　　**Carbs:** 0.3g　　**Fat:** 14.2g

Parmesan Pork Chops

Serves: 4

Prep Time: 15 mins.

Cooking Time: 9 mins.

Ingredients:

- 55 grams Parmesan cheese, grated
- 1 teaspoon garlic powder
- Salt and ground black pepper, as required
- 2 tablespoons olive oil
- 1 teaspoon paprika
- 1 teaspoon onion powder
- 4 (113-grams) boneless pork chops

Directions:
In a large shallow bowl, mix together the cheese and spices. Brush the chops with oil evenly and then coat with cheese mixture. Set the temperature of Air Fryer to 190 degrees C and preheat for 5 minutes. Arrange the chops into the air fryer basket. Slide the basket in Air Fryer and set the time for 9 minutes. Flip the chops once halfway through. Serve hot.

Calories: 266   **Protein: 34.9g**   **Carbs: 1.3g**   **Fat: 13.6g**

Pork Taco Casserole

Serves: 6

Prep Time: 10 mins.

Cooking Time: 25 mins.

Ingredients:

- 910 grams ground pork
- 115 grams cheddar cheese, shredded
- 260 grams salsa
- 2 tablespoons taco seasoning
- 225 grams cottage cheese

Directions:
In a bowl, add the beef and taco seasoning and mix well. Add the cheeses and salsa and stir to combine. Place the mixture into a baking pan evenly. Set the temperature of Air Fryer to 200 degrees C and preheat for 5 minutes. Arrange the baking pan into the air fryer basket. Slide the basket in Air Fryer and set the time for 25 minutes. Remove from Air Fryer and place the baking pan aside for about 5 minutes before serving. Divide the casserole into desired-sized pieces and serve.

Calories: 345   **Protein:** 50.3g   **Carbs:** 5.4g   **Fat:** 12.5g

Almond Coated Rack of Lamb

Serves: 6

Prep Time: 15 mins.

Cooking Time: 35 mins.

Ingredients:

- 795 grams grass-fed rack of lamb
- 1 organic egg
- 85 grams almonds, chopped finely
- Salt and ground black pepper, as required
- 1 tablespoon pork rinds, crushed

Directions:
Season the rack of lamb with salt and black pepper evenly and then drizzle with cooking spray. In a shallow dish, beat the egg. In another shallow dish mix together pork rinds and almonds. Dip the rack of lamb in egg and then coat with the almond mixture. Set the temperature of Air Fryer to 105 degrees C and preheat for 5 minutes. Arrange the rack of lamb into the greased air fryer basket. Slide the basket in Air Fryer and set the time for 30 minutes. Now, set the temperature of Air Fryer to 200 degrees C for 5 minutes. Serve hot.

Calories: 322 **Protein:** 31.6g **Carbs:** 3.1g **Fat:** 20g

Buttered Trout

Serves: 2

Prep Time: 10 mins.

Cooking Time: 10 mins.

Ingredients:
2 (150-grams) trout fillets
1 tablespoon butter, melted

Salt and ground black pepper, as required

Directions:
Season each trout fillet with salt and black pepper and then coat with the butter. Set the temperature of Air Fryer to 185 degrees C and preheat for 5 minutes. Arrange the trout fillets into the greased air fryer basket. Slide the basket in Air Fryer and set the time for 10 minutes. Flip the fillets once halfway through. Serve hot.

Calories: 374   **Protein:** 45.4g   **Carbs:** 0g   **Fat:** 20.2g

Haddock with Pesto

Serves: 2

Prep Time: 15 mins.

Cooking Time: 8 mins.

Ingredients:

- 2 (150-grams) haddock fillets
- Salt and ground black pepper, as required
- 3 tablespoons fresh basil, chopped
- 60 milliliters olive oil, divided
- 2 tablespoons pine nuts
- 1 tablespoon Parmesan cheese, grated

Directions:
Coat the fish fillets with 1 tablespoon of oil and then sprinkle with salt and black pepper. Set the temperature of Air Fryer to 180 degrees C and preheat for 5 minutes. Arrange the fish fillets into the greased air fryer basket. Slide the basket in Air Fryer and set the time for 8 minutes. Meanwhile, for the pesto: add the remaining ingredients in a food processor and pulse until smooth. Remove from Air Fryer and transfer the flounder fillets onto serving plates. Top with the pesto and serve.

Calories: 440   **Protein:** 38.2g   **Carbs:** 1.7g   **Fat:** 37.5g

Cheesy Shrimp

Serves: 6

Prep Time: 15 mins.

Cooking Time: 20 mins.

Ingredients:

- 76 grams Parmesan cheese, grated
- 2 tablespoons olive oil
- ½ teaspoon dried oregano
- ½ teaspoon red pepper flakes, crushed
- 910 grams shrimp, peeled and deveined
- 4 garlic cloves, minced
- 1 teaspoon dried basil
- 1 teaspoon onion powder
- Ground black pepper, as required
- 2 tablespoons fresh lemon juice

Directions:
In a large bowl, mix together the Parmesan cheese, garlic, oil, herbs, and spices. Add the shrimp and toss to coat. Set the temperature of Air Fryer to 175 degrees C and preheat for 5 minutes. Arrange the shrimp into the greased air fryer basket. Slide the basket in Air Fryer and set the time for 10 minutes. Remove from Air Fryer and transfer the shrimp onto serving plates. Drizzle with lemon juice and serve immediately.

Calories: 267   **Protein:** 38.9g   **Carbs:** 4g   **Fat:** 10g

Scallops with Capers Sauce

Serves: 2

Prep Time: 15 mins.

Cooking Time: 6 mins.

Ingredients:

- 283 grams sea scallops, cleaned
- 60 milliliters extra-virgin olive oil
- 2 teaspoons capers, finely chopped
- ½ teaspoon garlic, finely chopped
- Salt and ground black pepper, as required
- 2 tablespoons fresh parsley, finely chopped
- 1 teaspoon fresh lemon zest, finely grated

Directions:
Season each scallop evenly with salt and black pepper. Set the temperature of Air Fryer to 205 degrees C and preheat for 5 minutes. Arrange the scallops into the greased air fryer basket in a single layer. Slide the basket in Air Fryer and set the time for 6 minutes. Meanwhile, for the sauce: in a bowl, mix together the remaining ingredients. Remove from Air Fryer and transfer the scallops onto serving plates. Top with the sauce and serve immediately.

Calories: 372 **Protein:** 24g **Carbs:** 4.2g **Fat:** 29.5g

Jalapeño Poppers

Serves: 6

Prep Time: 15 mins.

Cooking Time: 13 mins.

Ingredients:

- 12 large jalapeño peppers
- 25 grams green onion, chopped
- ¼ teaspoon onion powder
- Salt, as required
- 226 grams cream cheese, softened
- 4 tablespoons fresh cilantro, chopped
- ¼ teaspoon garlic powder
- 44 grams sharp cheddar cheese, grated

Directions:
Carefully cut off one-third of each pepper lengthwise and then scoop out the seeds and membranes. In a bowl, mix together the cream cheese, green onion, cilantro, spices and salt. Stuff each pepper with the cream cheese mixture and top with cheese. Set the temperature of Air Fryer to 205 degrees C and preheat for 5 minutes. Arrange the jalapeño peppers into the air fryer basket. Slide the basket in Air Fryer and set the time for 13 minutes. Serve immediately.

Calories: 175   **Protein:** 5.2g   **Carbs:** 3.6g   **Fat:** 16g

Cranberry Muffins

Serves: 8

Prep Time: 15 mins.

Cooking Time: 15 mins.

Ingredients:

- 120 milliliters unsweetened almond milk
- ½ teaspoon organic vanilla extract
- 50 grams Erythritol
- ¼ teaspoon ground cinnamon
- 50 grams fresh cranberries
- 2 large organic eggs
- 150 grams almond flour
- 1 teaspoon organic baking powder
- 1/8 teaspoon salt
- 25 grams walnuts, chopped

Directions:
In a blender, add the almond milk, eggs and vanilla extract and pulse for about 20-30 seconds. Add the almond flour, Erythritol, baking powder, cinnamon and salt and pulse for about 30-45 seconds or until well blended. Transfer the mixture into a bowl. Gently fold in half of the cranberries and walnuts. Place the mixture into 8 silicone muffin cups and top each with remaining cranberries. Set the temperature of Air Fryer to 160 degrees C and preheat for 5 minutes. Arrange the muffin cups into the air fryer basket. Slide the basket in Air Fryer and set the time for 15 minutes. Remove from the Air Fryer and place the muffin molds onto a wire rack to cool for about 10 minutes. Carefully invert the muffins onto the wire rack to completely cool before serving.

Calories: 157   **Protein:** 2.4g   **Carbs:** 4.6g   **Fat:** 12.7g

Brownie Cake

Serves: 6

Prep Time: 15 mins.

Cooking Time: 35 mins.

Ingredients:

- 80 grams dark unsweetened chocolate chips
- 3 organic eggs
- 1 teaspoon organic vanilla extract
- 113 grams butter
- 50 grams Erythritol

Directions:

In a microwave-safe bowl, add the chocolate chips and butter and microwave for about 1 minute, stirring after every 20 seconds. Remove from the microwave and stir well. In a bowl, add the eggs, Erythritol and vanilla extract and beat until light and frothy. Slowly, add the chocolate mixture and beat again until well combined. Place the mixture into a lightly greased springform pan. Set the temperature of Air Fryer to 175 degrees C and preheat for 5 minutes. Arrange the cake pan into the air fryer basket. Slide the basket in Air Fryer and set the time for 35 minutes. Remove from the Air Fryer and place the pan onto a wire rack to cool for about 10 minutes. Carefully invert the cake onto the wire rack to cool completely. Cut into desired-sized slices and serve.

Calories: 257   **Protein:** 4.7g   **Carbs:** 3.8g   **Fat:** 24.6g

Cheesecake Bites

Serves: 12

Prep Time: 15 mins.

Cooking Time: 2 mins.

Ingredients:

- 226 grams cream cheese, softened
- 4 tablespoons heavy cream, divided
- 50 grams almond flour
- 125 grams Erythritol, divided
- ½ teaspoon organic vanilla extract

Directions:
In a bowl of a stand mixer, fitted with paddle attachment, add the cream cheese, 100 grams of Erythritol, 2 tablespoons of heavy cream and vanilla extract and beat until smooth. With a scooper, scoop the mixture onto a parchment paper-lined baking sheet. Freeze for about 30 minutes or until firm. In a small bowl, place the remaining cream. In another small bowl, add the almond flour and remaining Erythritol and mix well. Dip each cheesecake bite in cream and then coat with the flour mixture. Set the temperature of Air Fryer to 150 degrees C and preheat for 5 minutes. Arrange the cheesecake bites into the air fryer basket. Slide the basket in Air Fryer and set the time for 2 minutes. Remove from the Air Fryer and transfer the cheesecake bites onto a platter. Serve warm.

Calories: 109 **Protein: 1.5g** **Carbs: 1.4g** **Fat: 10.5g**

Printed in Great Britain
by Amazon